# Seeds of
# Success

# Seeds of Success

## 17 WAYS TO NURTURE THE GREATNESS WITHIN YOU

SHERYL TOWERS

PELICAN PUBLISHING COMPANY
GRETNA 2009

*The word "Pelican" and the depiction of a pelican are trademarks
of Pelican Publishing Company, Inc., and are registered in the
U.S. Patent and Trademark Office.*

**Library of Congress Cataloging-in-Publication Data**

Towers, Sheryl.
   Seeds of success : 17 ways to nurture the greatness within
you / by Sheryl Towers.
      p. cm.
   ISBN 978-1-58980-683-2 (hardcover : alk. paper) 1. Success.
2. Self-realization. 3. Self-actualization (Psychology) I. Title.
   BF637.S8T625 2009
   158.1—dc22

                                2009037762

Printed in the United States of America

Published by Pelican Publishing Company, Inc.
1000 Burmaster Street, Gretna, Louisiana 70053

*To my son, Justin*

# Contents

# Acknowledgments

I wish to express my heartfelt thanks to Mary Beth Gumbart, whose consistent encouragement, patience, and remarkable talent made this book possible. I am deeply grateful for your labor of love. Without you, this book would not exist.

I extend my deepest gratitude to Ellen Bush, Pamela Englebert, Rosalind McMillan, Karen Shockley, Kay Shurden, and Mary Wilder who evaluated the ideas, concepts, and early drafts of this book. Your insightful suggestions and feedback were invaluable. Thanks also to Robin Krueger, Carol Krueger, and Martha Jones.

Thank you to Matthew Michael and Mary Robinson for your very important last-minute advice.

Thank you to all the women spanning our thirteen years of study groups—your support is invaluable and appreciated beyond measure.

Thank you to the many clients and students who taught me so much and encouraged me to write this book. And to all the teachers and teachings that have contributed to my life, I am deeply indebted to each of you.

Finally, to my family and friends for your unending support and love, I am forever grateful. This book clearly would not have happened without you. Thank you for believing in me.

# Introduction

*"Though I do not believe that a plant will spring up where no seed has been, I have great faith in a seed. Convince me that you have a seed there, and I am prepared to expect wonders."*

—Henry David Thoreau

The twenty years that I have worked in the field of personal development have taught me that many of us have a diminished view of who we are, or what we can become. We seem to be out of touch with the vast potential and power within us, or we think that the help we need lies far outside of us. We often need a reminder of our tremendous possibilities . . . a reminder that the seeds of success are within each of us just waiting to blossom into a life of extraordinary fulfillment. Just as the oak tree is already imagined in the acorn, each of us has the potential to grow into a mighty force, finding ways and means of overcoming all obstacles. Both the height to which we soar and the way our future unfolds depend on how we cultivate these seeds.

If we cultivate these seeds of success with our imagination and water them with our faith, they will germinate, grow, flower, and bring forth fruits that will not only bless us, but also all of humanity. This growth starts with opening our minds and hearts to realize our possibilities, to see the possibilities inherent in all things. In the words of Ralph Waldo Emerson, "What lies behind us and what lies before us are tiny matters compared to what lies within us."

For many years, my possibilities felt limited and unreachable. Living a life of extraordinary fulfillment and contribution seemed beyond my capabilities. My heart has always been full of dreams, yet translating those dreams into reality felt like an impossible task. Like so many people, I came from a wounded past. I grew up with a profound sense of insecurity and inadequacy in a family where there was a lot of pain and violence. It was a traumatic, stressful life and one of huge unpredictability. It wasn't easy to convince myself that whatever my circumstances, I could always change my life by changing my mind. In my mind, success—even the most basic success of having enough money to pay my bills—was akin to rolling large boulders uphill.

Thus, the starting point for me toward a successful life was generating the belief that a more expressive, abundant life was even possible. I had to believe absolutely that I had the power to orchestrate my own success. I had to become totally willing to break free of the patterns that blocked me from living a rewarding and thriving life. The bottom line was that I had to break the boundaries of my own negative conditioning and learn to trust my dreams and intuition.

My journey of breaking my internal boundaries started on a chilly October night in 1981. Exhausted and distraught, I arrived at the doorsteps of my brother's home with thirty dollars in my pocket, three boxes of clothes, and my three-year-old son. I had left my Orlando home in fear and haste, never to return. It was an act of survival in a dangerous situation, a situation I later understood to be an unconscious re-creation of familiar childhood pain and patterns. A friend had slipped the thirty dollars into my pocket as we hugged good-bye. During the eight-hour drive to my hometown, I cried nonstop. The pain felt unbearable. My mind had let go, but not my heart. I was leaving behind my home, my belongings, my friends, my job, my marriage, and so many dreams. I was starting over.

Tucked in my purse was a little book by Mary Katharine MacDougall that I had picked up at a church bookstore entitled *What Treasure Mapping Can Do For You*. For the next few weeks, I followed MacDougall's advice and spent every possible moment browsing through magazines and brochures searching and clipping images that portrayed my deepest desires. I took these images and pasted them on poster board, making my "pictured prayers," and I found that they filled me with hope as I looked at them for years to come. These actions were certainly an act of faith for me, as I was plagued with a deep sense of helplessness and hopelessness. Yet amid the feelings of despair, I believed in God, and I believed God would help me if I would just do my part.

During this time, I dreamed of working through my troubles and creating a wonderful life for my son and me, and then writing a book of hope for others. This period marked the beginning of a long, difficult, and sometimes overwhelming journey that has proven to be infinitely rewarding.

Creating a new positive image of myself and coming to believe that I am indeed a worthwhile, valuable person took many years of hard work. Though I often wore a mask of joviality and confidence that perhaps fooled others, deep inside I felt sad and depressed. The truth was that I was filled with self-hate but did not know it as such. Only after years of probing my mind to see just where, when, and how this whole chain of destructive thoughts began, I came to understand the lack of regard that I had for myself.

The study of psychology offered tremendous help in stabilizing my emotional tensions. But I must say that a deeper sense of peace and joy in living came only when, through prayer and meditation, I began to experience my oneness with God. I was then able to embrace my own goodness and to know myself as an expression of God's love. As David Richo writes in his wonderful book *How to Be an Adult,* "By psychological work we are *changed.* In spiritual work we are *revealed:* we manifest our inner wholeness in conscious daily life."

Through psychological and spiritual work, I have moved through depression, despair, self-hate, poverty, and panic to a life filled with joy, love, purpose, beauty, comfort, and fulfillment. So many of my "pictured prayers" have come true. I love my life and thank God everyday for the miracles that have occurred. I also credit myself with working very hard to break through the limiting patterns that kept me from the joy and abundance that life has to offer.

I had many lessons to learn before I experienced the joy I so deeply desired. I had to learn to accept 100 percent responsibility for my life and to say "Yes" to my own needs. I had to learn discipline, not only discipline with my behavior, but with my thoughts as well. I had to learn to break the bondage of poverty that, with my belief systems, was holding me hostage. Perhaps the greatest lessons of all were those of learning to trust, to love, and to forgive both others and myself.

It is within reach for each of us to be the successful, blossoming expressions of love, life, wisdom, and joy that we are all designed to be. Just as a seed is full of promise with the beginning of a new life curled up inside, so it is with each of us. This very moment is a fresh new opportunity, and the possibilities are infinite. It is important to remember, however, that seeds need to grow at their own pace, and they will flourish at precisely the right time. Patience is a powerful tool. Have patience as your seeds grow and blossom, with a willingness to learn what you need to learn each step of the way and a commitment to nurture consistently these precious embryos.

We were born to flourish, to express our gifts to the

world. And the world certainly needs all the good we have to offer. Each of us has an opportunity to contribute to the evolution of humankind and the planet as a whole. Each of us has an opportunity to make this world a better place not only for ourselves, but for our children and grandchildren. In the words of George Bernard Shaw, "Life is not a 'brief candle'. It is a splendid torch that I want to make burn as brightly as possible before handing it on to future generations."

Across history, stories abound of people who committed to burning their torch as brightly as possible and thus creating a better world for all of us. Listening and learning from their success is motivating and healing. In this book, you will find stories of people from all generations and walks of life who lived their values and made their dreams come true. Like the sun's rays that cause the seed to stir within its husk, the energy of their passionate desires penetrated their soul, calling forth the courage within them. These bold people have inspired me to nurture the seeds of success within me and to envision more for my life. I hope they will inspire you.

It is my hope that in sharing some of the details of my life, as well as the stories of others, that I offer encouragement and support in the rekindling of your dreams. This book doesn't contain new information, just reminders of the wisdom you already possess. You will read what has been said before, but perhaps it can acquire new meaning for you as your circumstances change and your consciousness grows. Perhaps each time you hear an idea, you will hear it with a new awareness. Maybe, at some point, the bulb will go on in your head and you will know what is possible for you. Then, you will become unstoppable, and the seeds of success within you will grow to great heights.

# Seeds of
# Success

# 1

# Defining What Success Means to You

*"All that is required now is that you continue to till the soil of your soul. Just as you would not neglect seeds that you planted with the hope that they will bear vegetables and fruits and flowers, so you must attend to and nourish the garden of your becoming."*
—Jean Houston, *A Passion for the Possible*

At the end of my life, I want to know that I did all I could with all I had. The thought of looking back on a life of unrealized dreams is painful. I want to know that I had the courage to be who I truly am and that I made every effort to fulfill my potential. I want to know that I contributed something to the betterment of humankind. To me, this would be success. Benjamin Franklin said, "The noblest question in the world is, 'What good may I do in it?'" I love this idea. It inspires me to think about the meaning of my life.

We have an inborn urge to find meaning in life. We know that life must be more than mere existence; it must be more than how much we can accomplish or acquire. We want to feel that everyday we are moving toward our inherent potential. For most of us, living a successful life means living a life of purpose and contribution, which brings a keen sense of fulfillment. Finding that sense of purpose often means asking questions. So I ask you, what would you like to contribute to the world? What would you like to give back as a token of gratitude for having been given the gift of life? What difference would you like to have made in the lives of those you love?

To be involved in a continuing quest for deeper meaning and significance in everything we do shapes our life in a most powerful way, for the purpose of life is a life of purpose. This seeking of a purposeful life usually leads to being devoted to some cause outside of ourselves and larger than ourselves. Otherwise, we tend to be completely engrossed with our own immediate gratifications and lead self-centered lives. We then yield to societal pressures that make us obsessed with our possessions, our climb to the top, our appearance, or the size of our bank account. Without a purpose above and beyond our own individual pleasures and desires, we rarely find the satisfaction we so desperately seek.

When our external successes aren't connected to a significant purpose and therefore fail to bring the fulfillment we anticipated, we can find ourselves sinking into unhappiness. Or when we have outer success without being connected to our inner self, we may find ourselves feeling empty and unfulfilled. Sometimes those who appear to be successful on the outside are flooded with anxiety and emotional pain on the inside. Is this true for you? How do you feel about who you are and what you have done with your life? Do you have peace and joy in your life as it is while at the same time endeavoring for change and seeking growth?

Perchance there are areas of your life in which you feel very successful and other areas in which you feel incomplete. It may be that your career is a huge success, but other dreams were abandoned in the process. Or it may be that you have gotten your life shaped up the way you thought you wanted, and yet something doesn't feel right. You have made it to the top of the mountain and find that the view doesn't quite hold the thrill you envisioned. You have finally reaped the fruits of your labor only to find them less sweet than you imagined them to be. So you find yourself still dissatisfied and searching.

Maybe you have begun to understand that there is more to life than increasing its speed, and you recognize that an endless cycle of blind achievement will not lead to true fulfillment. A few years ago, I found myself at this point when I realized that I was living my life more as a compulsive and tiring trek filled with anxiety than as an exciting and often mysterious journey. This realization prompted me to change my view of success. It now means allowing my dreams and goals to enrich my life rather than making daily living more demanding.

Wherever you are on your journey, you can make a conscious decision to create your own definition of success and live your dream. You can make the decision to confront any limiting beliefs about who you are and what you are capable of so that you expand your vision. You can make an unalterable determination to manifest the deepest desires of your heart, and as you do, you will nurture the seeds of success within you.

Have you suppressed your own deepest wishes and desires? Are the dreams of what you truly want buried and in need of being rediscovered and identified? If so, allow them to surface. Consider that possibly you have been given dreams so that you may become aware of your talent, for your dreams contain the seeds of their own fulfillment. Your desire can be your compass. Your urge to succeed and your discontent in a given area is your intuitive awareness of something within you that wants to express itself.

Perhaps you know your dream and already possess a profound sense of readiness to make it a reality. Intellectually, you know that life is much too short to spend it doing something you truly don't enjoy. You know that the days that really count are the ones you experience with your heart. So you are ready. You are ready to resurrect old hopes and longings and express your true self. You are open to releasing old ways of thinking and behaving that restrict and stop you from being who you truly are.

I write this book in the hope of affirming that possibility for you. I know that for me books have always been such a source of motivation and comfort. For so many years when I was feeling lost, depressed, and lacking the courage to act on my dreams, I searched for books that offered hope. I could read and suddenly feel a surge of energy and inspiration, so from early on I had a voracious appetite for reading. That habit changed my awareness of life and myself. When nothing else could reach me, a good book would provide just the encouragement I needed. Books helped me to find my way and filled me with possibilities.

In my loneliness, books provided a refuge in the private lives of people who had triumphed over great odds. One of my earliest heroes was Mary Harris Jones, better known as Mother Jones. Here was a woman who lived through the Civil War, and just two years after it ended, lost her husband and four children in a terrible tragedy. In the midst of this, Mother Jones moved forward with her life, helping and comforting others. Tragedy struck again four years later when she lost everything she owned in the Great Fire that swept Chicago.

Any of these traumas would have been more than enough to emotionally destroy any of us. However, what did Mother Jones end up doing with her life? She fought for the rights of miners, railroad workers, and factory workers. In 1903, with mill children marching with her, she led a twenty-day protest march against child labor some 125 miles to see the president of the United States. She was the catalyst for child labor reform. Where Mother Jones's amazing response to loss came from, I do not know. But I do know that it was a powerful one that changed the course of history and offered countless people a better life.

My hope for a better life came through books that told the stories of people like Mother Jones. As Sarah Ban Breathnach uniquely expressed in her book *Simple*

*Abundance,* "Books are as essential as breathing. In my experience, when going down for the third time, it was often word-to-word resuscitation that saved the day." Similar to Breathnach's experiences, I can remember one night as a young woman feeling particularly desperate and defeated when I picked up a self-help book and read these words: "If anyone can succeed, and millions do, so can you. Believe, really believe, you can succeed and you will." Those words got my attention. Something inside me shifted. I had always said that I wanted to be successful, but did I really believe I could be? If success started with my deep-seated beliefs, where was I really?

My circumstances at that time revealed the answer to that question even if I wanted to deny the truth. Therefore, I decided to change my beliefs, to cling to that part of me which knew that I did indeed have an opportunity for success in my life; and I began to nurture its growth. Through a relentless commitment to develop my potential, I created a greater image of myself and for myself. As will be revealed in the chapters ahead, my journey to the core beliefs that were beneath my outer problems and unhappiness and to make conscious that which was unconscious was long, and continues to this day.

Through the process of exploring my inner world, an extraordinary fund of self-deprecation was exposed. I began to realize that so much of my energy was continually directed to pleasing more and more people in order to win more praise and ward off feelings of intolerable self-rejection. Even my initial approaches to change my life were about accomplishments that would also generate praise and approval. Thus, I found myself in the trap of experiencing success only when it came from the "outside-in."

Since accolades from the world represented success to me, there was never enough. I could love myself only if I performed well, so you can imagine how attached I was to the results of my efforts. I was unwittingly focused on recognition and glory, because as Julia Cameron says in *The Artist's Way*, "Fame is really a shortcut for self-approval."

Finally, I was able to understand the difference between true success and my ego's need for recognition and glory. It became very clear that merely collecting people and objects is not success. When I stopped fooling myself, I released those goals I was pursuing primarily for the praise they brought and began paying attention to my innermost needs. I stopped trying to be a member of so many different organizations, stopped trying to be friends with everyone who wanted to be "friends," and stopped trying to be in the limelight at every possible opportunity.

I put the brakes on, took inventory of my activities and priorities, and slowed down. I dropped the habit of rushing and conquering. It took some time to figure out what was truly rewarding to me, to gain the courage to live life on my own terms, to establish new goals that felt more like joyful challenges rather than grinding obsessions. For years, I had been involved in producing and hosting a community television show, and I decided to let that go in order to have more leisure time. I was compulsively attending aerobics classes, but I realized evening walks were more nurturing. I developed an interest in gardening and began to piddle around in my yard on the weekends. Eventually I allowed the standard of success in my life to be the amount of joy I felt on a daily basis.

I experienced a new enthusiasm for life when I decided to explore new interests, attempt new creative endeavors, and learn the things that had always been near and dear to my heart but would not necessarily win praise and recognition. Thus, I came to understand that the process of pursuing my dreams should be rewarding on its own terms—it's the journey that is most important. And on that journey, it's not what we get that makes us successful; it is what we become.

I found it enormously liberating to create my own definition of success. And that is exactly what I encourage you to do. Consider what represents true success to you. What are the longings of your heart, the aspirations of your mind? Consider them well, for they reveal your God-given gifts. They are the voice of your authentic self yearning for expression. It is essential that we learn to listen to our intuitive proddings, to honor our own desires, to honor our own life. It is essential that we treat our talents with love, respect, and care. Too many of us have believed that following our own bliss is a decadent sort of thing, or that the price we are required to pay is too high. The price that is actually too high to pay is to die with our dreams unfulfilled.

What is your unique dream, your unique talent? How are you sharing that special gift with the world? If you know your talent and you are sharing it with others, chances are you feel your life is on an upward spiral, continually getting better and better. If you are not owning your talent, sharing it, or going after what you love, there is typically a conflict connected with it. Look at that conflict. Is there a part of you that is afraid to become who you desire to be? Is there a part of you still frightened to follow your own path for fear of disappointing others? Trying to live up to the expectations of others robs our own sense of personal fulfillment.

Successful people follow independent paths. Asked once how she had developed her unique style, artist Georgia O'Keefe said, "I thought someone could tell me how to paint a landscape, but I never found that person. They could tell you how they painted their landscape, but they couldn't tell me how to paint mine." I encourage you to create your own definition of success so that it is intrinsic to the real you and discover your own vision about life. Commit to creating a life of your own without worrying about other people's judgments. This is the gateway to freedom.

Give yourself permission to venture out into the unknown, to examine new ideas with an open mind. Successful people dare to question what most people take as truth. Bold thinkers challenged such beliefs that the world was flat, or the sun revolved around the earth, or that evil spirits caused disease. The possibility of expanding your vision and enlarging your horizons always exists. Choose to become a possibility thinker.

In my introduction, I mentioned treasure maps as an important tool I've used in expanding my own personal vision. These maps fostered within me my own ability to become a possibility thinker. They helped me to use my imagination to create pictures of ideal conditions or events I want to experience. In the process of working on my maps, I slowly came to the realization that I was not given the ability to dream or given specific talents in order to be thwarted or frustrated. None of us are. Our dreams are guides to express our true self. Nothing we can dream of is too great for us to undertake if it hurts no one and brings happiness into our life. By fulfilling our own dreams, we often open doors for others. Such was the case for Clara Shortridge Foltz.

In California in 1878, a career in the legal profession was restricted to "male white citizen[s]," but Clara Foltz challenged that law. She lobbied for a bill allowing "woman lawyers" and was first to take advantage of the new legislation. Ten years earlier, Clara Foltz was barely surviving on an Iowa farm with two children and Jeremiah Foltz, whom she had married three years earlier at the age of fifteen. She later described herself as a "child-wife" married to a man who could not support his family; her life was a troubling one. Although her days were filled with manual labor, she allowed herself to acknowledge her longing for greater fulfillment in life, and she reached for it, making her dream come true.

A deeply alive place within you longs for fulfillment. I

urge you to find your own creative ways to identify and fill this innermost yearning. Doing so will rejuvenate your sense of wonder and delight, for pursuing your dreams puts joy in your soul and excitement in your life. Once you decide to follow your dreams, realize your goals, and reach for your own personal definition of success, you will feel an aliveness that fills you with passion. With a vision, there is passion, and passion is the most important ingredient in creating what you want.

A major tragedy of life would be never having the courage to act on your longings and create the life you want. Too often, we get half way through life and sadly realize that many of our hopes and deepest desires are still unrealized, and then we experience the emotional pain that unrealized dreams cause. We are so often frustrated and bored because of potentialities we have not expressed. We fail to reach our potential because we are hypnotized by the idea of being limited, and we shrink to fit our own limited perceptions. The truth is that the only one who can keep you from succeeding is you. When you open yourself to the belief that new and greater success will appear, you have taken the first crucial step.

I am so thankful that I opened to the belief that greater success could appear in my life. I opened to the realization that it takes just as much effort and energy to lead an unhappy life as it does to lead a happy, productive one. I am also thankful for having realized that most of the obstacles keeping me from making my dreams come true and expressing my authentic self to the world are internal and self-induced. In fact, many of these obstacles have much to do with habits.

Mastering your habits is a giant step toward creating a more powerful existence. In the chapters ahead, you will be encouraged to reflect upon where your habits are leading you and noting when old habits are running your life. You will be challenged to open to the possibility of changing those habits daily that don't serve you and embracing the idea that you can begin to change your life one habit at a time. By adopting new habits, such as writing affirmations, praying, journaling, exercising, reading your goals, and studying inspirational material, you enable the old to give way to the new.

As we change our habits, search for ways to challenge ourselves, and strive for something greater, we expand our sense of aliveness and happiness. We become excited about life and eager to contribute, and through our contributions, we make the world a better place. History proves that the positive impact one person's life can have on others is unquestionable. Ordinary human beings making extraordinary choices change the world. Margaret Mead reminded us: "Never doubt that a small group of thoughtful, committed citizens can change the world. Indeed it is the only thing that ever has."

The greatest people in the world are the thoughtful, committed citizens developing their own unique abilities and helping each other so that life might be better for all of us. They are not on the covers of magazines; they are in the middle of their communities serving, giving, and creating. They are dedicated to making a difference in their little corner of the world in a meaningful way. They are working not only to elevate their own life, but the lives of others as well.

As Henry David Thoreau said, "I know of no more encouraging fact than the unquestionable ability of man to elevate his life by conscious endeavor." By our own conscious endeavor, it is possible to live a way of life that takes us forward all the days of our life. In doing so, we nurture the seeds of success within.

## 2

# Accepting Responsibility

It is empowering to see yourself as a product of your choices rather than of circumstances. No one models this more beautifully than Maya Angelou, who has every reason to view herself as a victim of life. The injustices and heartaches she experienced as a young girl are far beyond what most of us experience in a lifetime. She survived the anguish of abandonment, sexual abuse, poverty, racial intolerance, and scores of other challenges that were constantly turning her world upside down. Not only did she survive, but she also developed a fierce dignity and strength.

I remember the emotion I felt watching Maya Angelou step up to the microphone at the inauguration of President Clinton to read her poem "On the Pulse of Morning." I sat in awe with my eyes glued to the television screen. She was the epitome of the "American Dream" and a phenomenal symbol of hope. By choosing not to be victimized by the overwhelming injustices she had experienced, she demonstrated for all of us the power of self-responsibility.

Unfortunately, not all of us follow Maya Angelou's example. It's amazing how we can refuse to be responsible for what is going on in our life. Regardless of how hurtful our behavior is to others and ourselves, we can always point the finger of blame at someone or something else. Instead of being responsible, we concoct ways to excuse or cover up our perceived failings and rationalize our deeds. We seek safety in the defenses of our ego, become reactive, and try to make others wrong. How easy it is to place the responsibility of our disappointments onto others.

Responsible people, however, don't point fingers of blame. They know that blame does not bring freedom. Instead, casting blame and refusing to be responsible lead to a heartbreaking cycle of failure and disappointment. Rather than making life easier, avoiding responsibility makes us less of a mature, successful person. How empowering it is to point the finger back at ourself in a spirit of compassion and curiosity. How empowering to stand on our own two feet and take full responsibility, reclaiming our own personal power to shape our life.

Our true power lies in honestly facing ourselves and taking responsibility for all aspects of our life. Unfortunately, many of us possess infantile attitudes about who is responsible for giving us what we want. Sometimes we find it easier to be sad, lonely, cynical, and suffering than to accept the challenge of making ourselves happy. Sometimes we wait to be rescued, hoping someone will come along and make our lives fun, comfortable, rich, exciting, or whatever we feel is missing. At other times, we allow other people to make our choices, not recognizing that it is indeed a choice to let others choose for us.

Taking personal responsibility for our choices is a habit. It is a habit that we can begin this very moment by being fully accountable for whatever is happening in our life and refusing to indulge in self-righteous victimhood. Taking personal responsibility means we no longer wallow in our circumstances wasting energy blaming people and things for holding us back. We can either see ourselves as victims of life or a life force. As the saying goes, "We can't control the wind, but we can control our sails."

Learning to control my sails has been a very challenging task, yet worth every moment of energy I expended and continue to expend in doing so. My life began to work when I learned to stop using blame as an excuse for why things were not exactly the way I wanted them to be, when I stopped using blame as a way to avoid the anxiety of self-examination. Focusing on why things were obviously someone else's fault prevented me from gaining the wisdom the experience presented. I needed to learn the lesson Shakespeare shared when he wrote, "The fault, dear Brutus, is not in our stars, but in ourselves."

It is easy to place blame elsewhere and to be comfortable in the role of victim when deep within we are conflicted by the pain of low self-worth. This was certainly true for me. For many years depression, confusion, and pain filled my inner world. To complicate matters, I was also angry with myself for feeling these negative emotions. I admonished myself for not being able to just get it together and feel good while at the same time pointing my blameful finger at others for their contribution to my unhappiness.

It wasn't until I connected with a loving, talented therapist, Dr. Gloria Lobnitz, that I began to gain some understanding of the pain within me. I began to see the connection between my low feelings of self-worth, my negative belief systems, and the circumstances of my life. I began to see that I unconsciously wanted to be rescued and to give my power away, because underneath my stoic exterior, I lacked confidence, and I was scared. I was also trying to escape feelings of failure.

Dr. Lobnitz immediately noticed my deep-seated belief that "something is wrong with me" and guided me in understanding how I had developed such a negative self-image. She was an angel in my life who steered me on the path of recovery and helped me to comprehend the impact of my childhood experiences. For the first time, I began to understand why I was in such an adversarial relationship with myself. Slowly I explored those patterns that prevented me from stepping up to the plate and taking full responsibility for my life.

But it was several years later that I came face to face with the hidden enemy, my self-hate, and the role it played in my unhealthy choices and in my tendency to blame.

After finding myself involved in yet another dysfunctional relationship, I sought the help of a wonderful psychiatrist, Dr. Bernard Williams. One afternoon, about six months after we had been working together, Dr. Williams looked at me and firmly said, "Today we are going to look at it." I was puzzled. "Look at what?" I asked. "We are going to look at how much you hate yourself." For a moment, I felt shocked and frozen. I had such an incredible act going on. How could he know? The truth was that on some level my act was fooling even me. Then suddenly I burst into tears and sobbed for an hour with such incredible pain pouring out of me. My secret was revealed. That evening I wrote in my journal, "A powerful session with Dr. Williams. The self-hate is being exposed."

Slowly I began to open to the possibility that on some level I create my own drama and suffering through my choices and through my hesitancy to be 100 percent responsible for the circumstances of my life. I saw that due to my lack of awareness, I had participated in the creation of so much pain in my life by making many unhealthy choices. I recognized how much energy I had spent in either making myself or someone else wrong and in nursing my emotional hurts. After recognizing these behavior patterns, I didn't *blame* myself—I just began to hold myself accountable.

Strangely enough, in looking back I can see that in some twisted way I believed struggling and suffering proved my goodness. I can remember telling my victim stories and feeling like such a noble person, not to mention the fact that I would become incredibly defensive if anyone even hinted that I might have some accountability in creating those events. My tendency was to blame my problems on others and to exonerate myself from accountability. I thank God and my wonderful counselors that my voice has become less bitter and defensive after years of personal healing work.

Until we stop blaming external circumstances for our unhappiness and accept responsibility for what is showing up, we cannot create the life of our dreams. We must accept that only we can make *ourselves* happy. To own that we are in charge of whether or not we are happy requires many of us to radically shift our way of thinking. Moreover, it requires working against cultural tendencies, for so much of our culture promotes blame, judgment, and excuses. To look at our possible contributions to our own frustrations, to be honest about our part in our problems, takes us out of our comfort zone, because it means letting go of our excuses and facing the consequences of our choices. This can be painful, so we often try to avoid looking at our role in our drama, creating crisis after crisis to avoid self-examination. However, the question to ask is: Do you want to live a life of excuses?

For most of us, the answer to that question would be a resounding "No." So how do we begin to take responsibility? The starting point is having the willingness to view what is truly going on in our life, to look at the way things *really* are. Sometimes we just don't want to face reality—the truth—because to do so would pressure us to make a decision or to take an action we don't want to take. So we avoid all information that conflicts with our view. But how often have we paid an even bigger price for not facing the truth?

Everyday we see people indulging in habits that threaten their health and quality of life, appearing not to care about the eventual consequences of their choices. There isn't a pack of cigarettes available that doesn't have a health warning, yet millions of people continue the habit. On a less obvious note are the scores of people who live in quiet desperation because certain relationships, or jobs, or activities in their life are no longer satisfying. Nonetheless, they continue to go along, not considering the impact their unhappiness has on their immune system. When you refuse to admit and accept what is happening in your life, you deprive yourself of peace, happiness, and optimal health. Once you face up to and accept responsibility for the parts of your life that aren't working, a new door of possibilities opens for you.

After examining your life, it is time to take the necessary action to alleviate or change the things that are not working. When you take action, you strengthen your sense of self and gain personal power. You can't just contemplate the problems in your life; you must do what ought to be done. Otherwise, you aren't living wisely. To live wisely, you must combine reflection with action.

In assuming total responsibility for your life through examination and action, it is essential to recognize when you blame others for how you are feeling. In assigning this blame, you give them the power to cause an emotional reaction inside of you. But when you take responsibility for your own feelings, the power comes back to you. This is most evident when you are holding bitterness or resentment and blaming the other person for "what they did" to you. Once you clearly claim your ability to choose a response that works for you regardless of "what they did," you are free.

If you have a lifelong pattern of allowing circumstances, events, people, and other factors outside yourself to disturb you and determine your feelings, it will be a challenge to claim your ability to control how you feel. Yet it is every bit worth the effort. Responding with awareness rather than reacting in the same old, unproductive or destructive patterns moves you forward. You can develop the habit of forming your own opinions about the things that occur, knowing that it is up to you to decide how to process and interpret them. For example, if your old pattern has been to react with defensiveness and anger at someone's judgment of you, you can choose not to take it personally. You can choose to give up the need to defend, to be right, or to make anyone wrong. You can also choose to respond with optimism when others around you are being gloomy and pessimistic. You don't have to jump into the sea of negativity.

You can feel your authentic feelings of sadness, anger, or fear without lapsing into the victim role. When you fall into the quicksand of self-pity or withdraw into your shell and feel sorry for yourself, you lose your power and only perpetuate your problem. Clinging to your suffering and complaining keeps you in your smallness. Complaining is self-defeating. The energy of people who are constant complainers and full of self-pity is repelling.

I became a single parent when my son was three years old. Child support stopped after the first year, and I felt like a victim. Since the role of victim was more familiar to me than that of a person who could take care of their self in the world, I was scared to give it up. I was simply terrified that I would not be able to provide for my son and me, so I hung onto my blame and anger. After much emotional anguish, I finally accepted the reality of the situation and summoned the courage to take full responsibility for our financial well-being. Then my life began to shift, and I began to see new possibilities.

In the process of creating this breakthrough for myself, I observed another unhealthy pattern in my life. This pattern had to do with what I call "waiting to be rescued," which meant investing huge amounts of energy into "being sweet" and "doing it right" for someone else in the hope that I would ultimately be taken care of. This behavior, of course, only left me filled with despair and resentment, as it always does when you give away your personal power.

Nevertheless, I spent a lot of time being "nice," and I often chose "nice" over honest. I felt too fearful of rejection and abandonment to express my desires and feelings honestly and assertively, so I stuffed most of them. Yet, I expected those close to me to be mind readers, which frustrated me when I didn't get what I wanted. After repeating this negative pattern over and over and getting the same results, I finally understood that being responsible involves the practice of assertiveness. Gradually, I began to speak my truth and to value my feelings. As I did so, those periodic aggressive outbursts that occurred when I could no longer stuff were eliminated.

The goal of assertiveness is not necessarily to get your way or to be victorious over others. It is about taking care of you. It is about being responsible for your own feelings, needs, and wants. It is about taking full responsibility for naming your needs and desires. Replacing passive behavior with assertive, self-valuing patterns is a giant step toward self-responsibility.

Through our daily choices of behavior and thought—to be more assertive, more honest, and more self-aware— we either squander our opportunities or develop our potential. We can use our gift of conscious choice to create a greater life for ourselves. Conscious choice means taking the consequences of our choices into consideration when making our decision. It means responding with the awareness and knowledge that the consequences are our own, the results of our own choice. Conscious choices lead to more responsible choices.

Responsible choices often necessitate changing certain types of habitual behavior and being willing to let go of old belief system. Letting go requires creating new scripts about life that give you permission to release any negative scripts you grew up with that limit you. Most of us have countless, almost unnoticed negative beliefs that work against us: "I can't handle money," or "I'll always be fat," or "Life is too hard," and on and on. These kinds of self-talk create the inner belief that life is a struggle; we, therefore, unconsciously create circumstances congruent with that belief.

You must take the responsibility of silencing the negative "self-talk." You can begin by identifying areas of your life in which you are having problems, for there will be a connection between those areas and your self-talk. What are you struggling with in your life? What is interfering with your being able to live your life the way you truly want? Struggle is primarily a programmed response; therefore, when we give ourselves new scripts and time to integrate those scripts, struggle can be seen in our life from a new perspective. It can then be viewed as old negative beliefs that had us experiencing life as a world of ever-recurring conflicts and discords. However, if we absolutely believe that struggle is a necessary part of our life, then it will be and will remain so.

When I was just beginning to understand this concept, I tried an experiment with myself. I chose to give up struggling for one entire day, which essentially meant stepping off the treadmill of worry and trusting life. I decided not to struggle with making happen everything I thought needed to happen: not to struggle with trying to be everything to everybody, not to struggle with trying to figure out why certain people were doing what they were doing, and on and on. I quickly discovered I was not a person who easily gives up struggling. My inner enemies met me full force, telling me I would get nowhere with such a "laid back" approach to life. They demanded that I resume control and make things happen. Giving up the struggle of trying to control everything was like going through withdrawal.

We may have to take the responsibility of letting go of many of the things we've been clinging to make room for the new. We may have to let go of our need to control. We may have to let go of old belief systems, as a change of mind always precedes a change of experience. And though we are infinitely changeable, it is often as Shakespeare wrote in *Hamlet.* We had "rather bear those ills we have than fly to others that we know not of." We bear the ills we have because our fears paralyze us and collapse our sense of possibilities.

Therapy was one of many tools I used to deal with my own paralyzing fears and to open to a greater sense of possibilities and self-responsibility. Learning how my fears had run me in my past empowered me to design a better future. But therapy wasn't the only tool. Imagery and positive self-talk were also powerful. I began thinking of myself as a human magnet, attracting to myself that to which I was mentally attuned. I realized that I had been so caught up in my fears and despondencies that I was attracting the negative—more troubles and miseries. With great determination, I learned to focus my mind on my goals and deepest desires with confidence, and as I did so, more of those positives came into my life.

Several years ago, I attended a workshop at Esalen Institute facilitated by Mary Goldenson, a gifted teacher and the author of *It's Time, No One's Coming to Save You.* Goldenson challenges us to step out from behind our defenses (those old adaptive patterns we developed to help us cope), to live from our heart, and to wake up to the greatness of each moment of life. She challenges us to take full responsibility now. After the workshop, I came home and made several changes in my life that I found enormously liberating, such as taking several initiatives about my finances and restructuring my business schedule. I finally got it, as Goldenson says, that no one was coming to save me!

Goldenson's workshop focused on the importance of designing one's life and making responsible choices. It reminded me that we are like beautiful pieces of marble sculpted by our own moment-to-moment choices. Our future is integrally connected to our willingness to be fully responsible for our minute decisions and with what we choose to do with our present opportunities. Our choices affect us in far-reaching ways. We are where we are because of our choices. And our choices write our autobiography for the future.

# 3

# Saying Yes to Your Own Needs and Enjoying the Moment

Years ago, as I sat in a workshop in Chicago facilitated by Dr. Bernie Siegel, I was filled with awe as I listened to the testimonials of individuals describing their miraculous recovery from a variety of illnesses. Instrumental in their recovery was their decision to make their own needs and care a priority. I listened intently as Dr. Siegel presented studies revealing that people who develop cancer are those who tend to be compulsive givers and are restricted in expressing emotions, particularly related to their own needs. He suggested that cancer might be called the "disease of nice people."

Hearing his words and the stories of those around me, I realized that lifelong patterns of self-denial can literally kill us. And I realized how much self-denial and stress had been created in my own life by constantly being on the lookout for what others thought of me. For the longest time I wasn't fully alive because I wasn't fully me. From early on, I felt some pressure to deny my true feelings, to be someone other than my true self. I was driven by the need to seek approval, believing that if I could convince other people of my accomplishments and become accepted by them, then I could accept myself and enjoy my life. I believed I had to earn the acceptance and love of others. Only then would I count for something.

I was afraid to change into who I really was because I feared that those close to me would not love or accept me anymore. I was afraid that if I stood up and expressed how I truly felt I would be rejected or abandoned. So I abandoned myself for acceptance and approval. I spent time with people who exhausted me, because I didn't want to "hurt anyone's feelings," and in doing so, I hurt myself and wasted my precious time. I continually gave my power away by craving the validation of others.

The philosopher Lao Tzu wrote, "Care about people's approval and you will be their prisoner." I lived as a prisoner for a very long time. Finally, my powerful drive for autonomy no longer allowed me to give up my authenticity for the comfort that comes from the approval of others or to preserve the status quo. I was tired of burying pieces of myself under my hunger for acceptance. I was weary of clinging to roles, relationships, and activities that I had outgrown. I began to step outside my comfort zone, to expose myself to people and situations that stretched me, and to develop a willingness to let go of the familiar. I began to let my life be re-created by the power within me, rather than the power of the world around me. Slowly, what I wanted began to shape more of my life than what I feared.

We have trouble accepting ourselves as we are when we are trying hard to be what others want us to be. Unfortunately, society programs us to fit in rather than to find out who we are. Yet, we are free to say yes to our own needs only when we can say no to societal pressures. I once heard Caroline Myss say, "We must unplug from those sources that we are losing so much power to so that we can plug into ourselves." Saying no to those sources, however, often produces uneasiness, and we are resistant to being uncomfortable. The truth is that continuous growth involves discomfort, for breaking boundaries can be very unsettling. Birthing ourselves into a new life brings labor pains.

A driving desire to belong to the group can deprive us of our true identity, for we learn to put on masks and play the roles we think others expect of us. We create a false self to mask our insecurities and sacrifice our true self for this "image." This hiding of who we are robs us of the joy of intimacy with others and ourselves. We find great freedom when we relinquish our need to have our worth validated by others.

Throughout history, people of great achievement have dealt with issues of breaking boundaries, escaping social demands, and pressing forward to say yes to their own needs. I shudder to think where we would be today if no one ever strayed from conformity. This breaking of boundaries has particularly been true for women who challenged societal norms and marched to their own beat. Sometimes frightened of unconventionality, but desperately needing to be themselves, these women took risks to reveal their hidden ideals and pursue their dreams. They often confronted issues of power and control because these traits were declared unwomanly. One such woman was Elizabeth Blackwell.

Elizabeth Blackwell dreamed of being a doctor at a time when women did not become doctors. After deciding to pursue her longing, she ran into strong prejudice and crushing opposition. Determined, she taught music during the day, read medical books at night, and sent application letters to all the major medical schools. Her letters were met with nothing but negative responses labeling her an "inappropriate" candidate. Finally, in 1847, she was accepted to Geneva Medical College, a small school in New York.

The school later confessed that the student body admitted her as a joke. However, no one was laughing on January 23, 1849, when she graduated with top honors as the first woman physician in the United States. Elizabeth Blackwell was a true pioneer who had the courage to be herself without worrying about other people's acceptance. She broke the boundaries, and her perseverance and determination helped women after her to realize their dreams. She clearly followed the advice of Robert Louis Stevenson: "To know what you prefer instead of humbly saying Amen to what the world tells you that you ought to prefer is to have kept your soul alive." So I ask you, what do you want most in life? What is your soul longing for? What is it that you have a deep need to do?

We are often afraid to ask for what we want, so answering those questions may be difficult. Our life experience has not demonstrated that we can have what we want, so we fear disappointment. I have a friend who expresses a great desire to earn a college degree but refuses to seriously entertain the idea of returning to school. Having failed several classes in her freshman year, she has a deep-seated fear of "making a fool of herself" by trying again. Yet, she lives with a great insecurity about being the least-educated person in her family. I have another acquaintance who says he wants an intimate relationship; however, he lives an isolated, lonely life. Many years ago, he experienced a painful betrayal, leaving him unwilling to risk being hurt again. In fact, he has almost silenced that voice of desire.

It can be very difficult to hear yourself when that self has been silenced for so long. If you don't practice listening to the truth of your inner needs, they will show up in negative ways, such as depression or addiction, to get your attention. Underground feelings will not just vanish. They will eventually cry out, even if you try to deny them. The crying out is usually so painful that you are almost forced to explore your feelings and needs. Why wait for these negative emotions to cry out? With an ongoing commitment to listen and honor your inner voice, you are less likely to experience these negative states.

I encourage you to begin thinking about what you want and to ask for it. Begin to say yes to your own needs. One of the signs of increasing emotional health is listening to your inner voice and spending less time denying your needs. Discover what your needs are and practice meeting them. The things in life you are most hungry for can only be given to you by you. Listen to the innate wisdom of your true self, to your intuition. It is one of your most valuable resources. Let it lead you to discover your deepest desires, for your desires are your compass.

If you want to be happy, you must practice following your heart and intuition. You must focus on living a life that is authentic and moves beyond trying to impress others. You must be willing to let go of any outdated versions of who people think you are and allow yourself to be the authority on what is good for you. You must examine your life, eliminate what isn't working, experiment and take risks, and create a life that you love. Otherwise, you will remain stuck and live what Thoreau called a life of "quiet desperation."

Don't be surprised if guilty feelings pop up when you begin to make your needs a priority. Just remind yourself that you deserve to be a priority in your own life and that you deserve to include yourself among the people to whom you wish to be kind and loving. You can know and express what you want without being greedy or self-centered. Saying yes to your own needs is vitally connected to what you offer to life. You can be a source of peace and joy for others only after you have taken the responsibility to bring peace and joy into your own life. Your own personal growth and self-care are central to all the help you provide to others. You can't love others well if you are constantly giving to others but failing to nurture yourself.

The people causing the greatest chaos in the world are those who neglect to nurture and care for themselves in healthy ways. They are often people who spend their time doing boring and depressing things, whose activities and achievements drain them. They may be invested in trying to stay safe rather than being adventurous or fully involved with life. Happy people are constantly expanding and experimenting and making positive contributions to the world. They take time to play and enjoy life, which causes their creative imagination to soar. Amazingly creative work is often birthed in fantasy and play.

We instinctively know that play is an essential part of life because of the joy it brings. Without joy, we aren't really living. Sadly, we often feel that we have lost our joy, or that we have lost something of tremendous value in the process of growing up. We miss that enthusiasm and simple trust we knew as a child. We miss feeling full of hope that something new and thrilling lies ahead. This loss of enthusiasm is a clue that it is time to reclaim those parts of ourselves we have long ago disenfranchised. It is time to claim our power to change our world and to bring as much play and joy as possible into our everyday life.

As you close the gap between how you spend your time and what is important and joyful to you, you will find your life more deeply satisfying. You will notice there is something enormously rejuvenating about opening your mouth and telling the truth about who you are, how you feel, and what you need and then acting upon it. You may also notice that as you choose to move into a fuller expression of your true self, parts of your life may begin to feel too constricting, like an outgrown garment. So you move on and leave some things behind. You summon the courage to let go of things that are no longer fulfilling.

You may reach a point where going back to who you used to be just won't work, nor will living a value system you've outgrown. You may find that participating in activities from which you received little pleasure is no longer necessary, because you now have the fortitude to say "no." Congratulate yourself, for in the words of E. E. Cummings, "It takes courage to grow up and turn out to be who we really are."

Summoning the courage to let go has been no easy task for me. So often my mind wanted to let go and move toward the future, but my heart felt stuck. I had such difficulty letting go of what needed to be left behind, such as relationships that no longer worked or activities that bored me. At the time, I didn't realize why I struggled so much, but now I think about Sarah Ban Breathnach's words in her wonderful book *Simple Abundance:* "The closer we get to giving our dream to the world, the fiercer the struggle becomes to bring it forth. Why should this be so? Because we will be inexorably changed, and life can never return to the way it once was."

Not only have these words presented their truth in my own life, I have witnessed their truth being played out in the lives of others. I watched as a friend in her mid-forties struggled with her dream of returning to school to study art though her husband was adamantly opposed. He felt it would rob them of time together. She felt it would give her a new zest for life and satisfy a deep longing. Now in school, she confided that she feels more fulfilled than ever, but her relationship with her husband has changed. She commented that her life "could never return to the way it once was," and she continues to be in the process of dealing with the changes in her marriage.

Taking the talent and potential we were born with and developing them does bring change, but they also bring a deep sense of fulfillment. And self-fulfillment brings such a sense of enthusiasm and joy and unleashes tremendous energy. So I ask you, what do you yearn to do—write, dance, help the needy, plant a garden, spend more time with your family, develop new friendships? What would it take to reawaken your sense of wonder? Do it. Allow your creative expression to flow into your everyday life. Continually cultivate your curiosity about life and find ways of surprising yourself and others every day. Zest, passion, spontaneity, and a sense of adventure soar as we allow our imagination to take flight in our daily life.

Letting go of our old habitual ways of doing things rejuvenates us. A change in even the simplest of habits such as the way we dress, style our hair, drive to work, spend our leisure time, or exercise can give us a renewed sense of vitality. Bigger changes such as a new career, a new circle of friends, a new home, or going back to school can enrich and enlarge our lives and give it more meaning.

One of the ways to rediscover our passion and renew ourselves is to engage in some pampering. Pampering is a healthy thing to do because it rejuvenates us. Some people feel guilty if they aren't doing "the sensible thing." However, like play, pampering has all sorts of psychological benefits, which include enhancing our creativity. This good self-care helps us release our frustrations and negative feelings, which encourages our spontaneous, creative self. As happy, fulfilled individuals, we are so much more loving to others and ourselves. So give yourself permission to have a massage, or some time in the steam bath, or a day of solitude, or a weekend away . . . whatever it takes to refresh your spirits.

Of course, some of us have difficulty playing or pampering ourselves because of the ongoing anxiety produced by our inner talk. That inner chatter says no matter what we are doing we should be doing something else. We think that if we are playing, we should be working. If we are working, we should be exercising. If we are exercising, we should be reading. And on and on it goes. Our anxieties and judgments so often keep us out of the moment, robbing us of joy. Life, however, was not meant to be about constantly performing and then judging our performance.

Saying yes to your own needs involves slowing down, so you can find joy in the most mundane things, and refusing to listen to that negative self-talk telling you what "you should be doing." Saying yes to your needs allows you to turn the chronic worry volume way down. Slowing down allows you to savor the gifts of each day, to take the time to listen to nature's music: the birds, the wind, the surf, the waterfall, the insects, and the many other melodies that surround us.

The kinds of life experiences that offer deep fulfillment aren't necessarily moments of obvious achievement or busy moments of doing. They are most often those instances of fully experiencing and enjoying exactly where you are and who you are. They might be watching a sunset, sitting quietly in nature, sharing a delicious meal, or just relishing the sheer delight of being alive. Whatever they might be, they are moments when you are completely and totally present, filling yourself up with love, meaning, and opportunity that are already there for you.

We can elevate the quality of our life by staying engaged in what we are doing at the moment and allowing that activity to arrest our attention, rather than rushing through or numbing out to the small facets of daily living. As vital as I believe having goals, plans, and ambitions are, I am no longer willing to allow them to diminish who I am today. I realize I can create feelings of joy and peace even if I haven't achieved all of my goals, even if things aren't perfect, even though I'm not perfect.

While writing this book, I reminded myself daily that the process was actually more important than the outcome. This awareness helped me to feel less compelled to rush to finish it. I knew that I would spend millions of minutes writing this book, and I wanted to enjoy each and every one. I wanted to experience the delight in its creation. I knew that I would become more than I was in the process of writing it.

We can choose to fully enjoy every moment as we consciously move in the direction of our goals. We can even choose to accept our moments of pain and sadness without being frightened by them. We can experience our anger without being trapped by it. We can pay attention to where our mind is, and when we find that considerable amounts of our energy are expended in anticipating, worrying, regretting, or planning what we want to happen or don't want to happen, we can choose to bring ourselves back to the present moment.

Our creative power actually exists in the present moment. If we can make the present moment all it can possibly be, moments in the future will take care of themselves. More importantly, if we don't live in the present moment, we may never get around to living at all. Life does not happen in the future. It happens right now. Life is created moment by moment in the minutest details, in the most ordinary activities of everyday life. There is a Sanskrit poem that says, "Each today, well-lived, makes yesterday a dream of happiness and each tomorrow a vision of hope. Look, therefore, to this one day, for it and it alone is life." Our greatest achievement is being able to live in the moment and feel peace within.

Barbara De Angelis expresses the importance of living in the moment when she writes in her book *Real Moments*,

> If you can't be happy now, with what you have and who you are, you will not be happy when you get what you think you want. If you don't know how to fully enjoy $500, you won't enjoy $5,000, or $500,000. If you can't fully enjoy taking a walk around the block with your mate, then you won't enjoy going to Hawaii, or to Paris. I'm not saying that having more money or more recreation won't make your life easier—it will. But it will not make you happy, because it can't. Only you can do that by learning to live with more real moments.

Being right here right now is a matter of training our mind, a matter of practicing. Make it a habit to notice things in your everyday life that you have typically taken for granted. Notice the colors, the fragrances, the textures, and the beauty of all that surrounds you. Wherever you are, be there. Live as fully as possible in the now with gratitude and respect. When the activities of our daily life become infused with a sense of reverence, we feel alive with meaning and purpose.

When we are experiencing ordinary life as rich and

miraculous, expressing our creativity, feeling passionate about what we do, and are being our authentic self, it is difficult not to succeed. Why? Because we are filled with passion, and passion fills us with the energy to manifest our dreams. It motivates us. Whether it's developing a business plan or writing poetry, raising children or owning a company, going back to school or moving to a new area, every deep desire arises from passion. If we see our life as the process of becoming more and conveying more of who we authentically are, then the passage of time can bring great joy.

Changing our focus from staying in our comfort zone to living with passion can give us renewed energy. Allowing change to happen in our life can be freeing, yet we gear so much of our energy toward trying to keep change from happening. The truth is that everything is in process; everything is always changing. But emotionally we have a difficult time accepting this. Often our refusal to let go indicates our disbelief that something greater lies ahead.

Instead, trust that as you take one step forward, the next step on your path will be revealed. Know that following your intuition often results in things coming together in what we sometimes call a synchronistic event. "Synchronicity" is a term coined by Carl Jung to describe the situation when events in our lives appear to happen in ways that seem to defy completely the laws of probability. In *The Structure and Dynamics of the Psyche,* Jung describes how, during his research into the phenomenon of the collective unconscious, he began to observe coincidences that were connected in such a meaningful way that their occurrence seemed to defy the calculations of probability.

For example, have you ever had some of these incidences happen to you: You have been thinking of someone and run into that person a few hours later? Perhaps someone you had not seen in years. Or maybe you've had a bill due for a certain amount, and that exact amount appears unexpectedly. Or maybe you are seeking the answer to a question when suddenly a book or person appears with the very information you need. We typically describe these events as chance encounters, but they very well might be evidence that our psyche connects at a deeper level to things outside itself, that the whole universe is more linked than we can imagine.

It seems to me that synchronicity is the universe's way of supporting us in having our heart's desire. It is a way of connecting us to the resources we need to have our gifts and talents used. By following our intuition and listening to our true self, we stay attuned to the synchronistic events that help us express the divine possibilities implanted in our mind and soul, leading us to the development of our great potential.

The seeds of success within you are just waiting to spring forth and grow. Your world is pregnant with possibility. It's time to say yes, for the world needs your genius. If you don't believe the world needs you, think of the magnificent differences that people such as Oprah Winfrey, Bill Gates, Jody Williams, Nelson Mandela, and many others have made. When you say yes to your own needs and celebrate every moment of your life, you will find that your creativity has the potential to enlarge not only your own consciousness, but also all of humanity. Consider how making your dream come true can be a blessing to others. Consider how discovering and developing your unique gifts cannot only satisfy you, but benefit the world.

# 4

# Balance

Recently I read an article in which an interviewer asked Tiger Woods to name the "secret" of his success in coping with the pressures of having emerged as one of the world's most famous athletes. Woods replied that to him it was all about balance. "I just try to keep everything as simple as possible and as balanced as possible. If I feel something is out of balance, I try to get it back in balance somehow. Your entire life, you're always working to keep everything in balance because the more harmony there is, the smoother life goes."

Woods, like most successful people, has learned the importance of living in a state of balance and harmony. Without balance, the quality of our life is greatly diminished. Without balance, things collapse and negative consequences occur. Overstaying our time in imbalance leads to exhaustion or "burnout" and depletes our sense of joy. We can be so-called successful people in the world doing powerful things, but if that feeling of peace, joy, and harmony does not fill our heart, then it's just not worth it.

Unfortunately, maintaining our balance isn't easy while living in a time of the most rapid change in human history. Nevertheless, balance is a key word in every area of our life, for to be effective in the world and to feel good about ourselves, it is necessary to nourish our body, mind, emotions, and spirit. Neglecting one area of our life causes the others to suffer. And unless success includes our whole being, it isn't the glittering prize it appears to be.

When each of these dimensions of our life—the spiritual,

mental, emotional, and physical—is fully integrated, we feel more stable and whole. Yet rarely do we invest equal amounts of energy in each, tending instead to pay special attention to those aspects that are most important to us and give us a greater sense of self-worth. It makes us vulnerable to base our sense of self-worth on an area of our life (such as a job, relationship, or particular skill), for we risk slipping into despair should something happen to undercut that component. It also makes us vulnerable to the consequences of neglect in the other areas.

I have a friend whose frame of reference about his value was almost totally related to his work and earning money. The majority of the time, he felt depleted and exhausted, and he suffered from chronic backaches and ulcers. He took little time to nurture or maintain relationships, engage in hobbies, or take care of his health. Yet, he was greatly applauded by his company as being hard working, responsible, and ambitious. Then he had a heart attack, and his worldview suddenly changed. He is now exploring healthier and more rewarding ways to gain a sense of purpose and value and to keep his life in balance. He is learning to applaud himself.

Not only do we risk jeopardizing our own well-being when our bodies reach a crisis level, but we also risk hurting others. For example, extreme fatigue has been increasingly claimed as the primary cause of many major accidents. A sleep-deprived Conrail employee working double shifts was controlling a train that crushed a railroad worker. Fatigue was also declared the root cause of the Exxon Valdez oil spill and the Three Mile Island nuclear power plant accident. These are but a few cases of fatigue-related accidents.

Approaching our days tired, tense, and frustrated creates many of the problems we experience in life. We overcommit, overfunction, overperform, and overappease, all of which leave us weary and worried. Then our stress and anxiousness on the inside produce problems and pressures on the outside. Pushing ourselves to extremes is exhausting and dangerous. We must learn to be careful custodians of our energy and refuse to take on more than our mind and body can handle.

Merely waiting for circumstances to improve will not work. You must decide to slow the speed at which your life is moving. You must begin to take action on behalf of your own health, happiness, and peace of mind. You must allow a healthy mind and body to be your first priority and commit to managing your life according to that priority. Otherwise, the quality of your life is greatly diminished. By honoring a soul-satisfying rhythm, you function better, experience more calmness, and enhance your health.

I have gone through cycles with my life feeling incredibly out of balance. Such was the case one spring when I decided to attend a retreat at the Himalayan Institute in Honesdale, Pennsylvania. Working full time, single parenting, attending graduate school, hosting a community television show, and heaven knows what else, I was near burnout. Therefore, the opportunity to participate in a stress-management seminar sounded very appealing to me.

Immediately upon my arrival, however, I quickly realized that when I signed up for this program, I had little idea of what was in store for me. It definitely was not going to be the type of seminar to which I had been accustomed. In fact, what I had actually involved myself in was a silence retreat referred to as a combined therapy program. The combined therapy meant a natural diet, breathing techniques, meditation, biofeedback, gentle exercises, and long periods of silence.

The accommodations were austere with, of course, no telephone, radio, television, or other outside distractions. I was told that meals would be served to me in my room, except for the meals provided at the beginning and end of the retreat, and even during those two occasions, meals would be observed in silence. I soon realized that being alone with myself for a long period with absolute silence was a very tough challenge.

Within a few days, utter panic and desperation began to well inside me, and I encountered the raw edges of my personality. In addition, I began to manifest severe physical symptoms from the sudden withdrawal of caffeine and sugar. I wanted to run away. I wanted to return to my hectic life and the drama to which I was accustomed. What I did not want was to feel the emotions that were bubbling up inside me. I wanted to push those feelings back down, because they were just too uncomfortable.

The greatest lesson I learned from this experience was the undeniable truth that so much of my stress is created by my own internal states. For most of my life, I had been blaming my stress on events and circumstances outside myself. But here I was in this incredibly beautiful environment with nothing requested of me but to relax and to be quiet, and I was becoming totally stressed out. It became very clear to me that if I didn't begin to take charge of my mind and emotions, they would take charge of me.

I also came to understand that underneath the conscious mind, we have layers of repressed issues, and all of these issues reside in our subconscious mind. When our minds are quiet, and when we allow ourselves to just *be*, this subconscious material manifests. Slowing down allows those pent-up emotions that have built up over time to rise to the surface. Most of us fill our lives with such distractions and busyness that we don't look at these suppressed things. We rush through our days with great speed, focusing on the more shallow aspects of our life.

The circumstances in which I found myself at the Himalayan Institute provided the very lessons I needed in order to expand my awareness and to see just how out of balance my life had become. I discovered the self-destructive pace at which I was pushing myself, fueled by wounds I had never allowed to heal or myself to feel. I discovered that behind my mask of success lurked disillusionment and fear. As I slowly let go of this mask, I experienced a deeper part of myself and became less driven by my fears and old hurts.

I am pleased to say that six years later, I attended a Zen Meditation Retreat, and it was an exhilarating experience. I loved the silence. I welcomed the time to be quiet, alone, and with myself. Now one of the absolute essentials in my life for my emotional and spiritual health is to have time alone, and I find the solitude glorious. Taking the time to disengage from everything and everyone nurtures my soul and allows me the splendor to listen to my own heart and mind. It gives me a chance to reestablish equilibrium and to return to life with more vitality.

Allowing ourselves precious moments to relax and re-vitalize rather than perform or entertain is essential, for without time for renewal, our deepest longings get lost in the frustrations and routines of daily life; and we lose touch with our inner life. Doing must be supplemented by being—looking inward, reflecting, questioning, wondering. Creating space to receive insight not available through action-oriented behavior is necessary. There is no substitute for the creative inspiration, knowledge, and stability that come from renewal, from taking quiet time to reenergize and refocus. It is in practicing solitude on a regular basis that we allow silence to be the great teacher that it is. We come to know ourself.

Allow yourself a period of nondoing at least once a day everyday of your life. Give yourself permission to pause, allowing impressions to sink in. Give yourself time to sense your feelings. When you get away from worldly activity and experience that consciousness of peace and bliss that is within you, it overflows into your outward activity and affects everything you do in a more positive way. Your consciousness changes and you become kinder, more loving, and more joyful.

Most of us are hungry to embrace more fulfilling ways of living. We often sense a need to move toward success in a way that is healthy, not succeeding at the expense of other areas of our life, or forfeiting our soul. Many of us are beginning to recognize that the "hurry syndrome," which is a national ailment, no longer works for us. Our busyness is making us sick. The Chinese word for "busy" is composed of two characters: "heart" and "killing," and too often we seem to be having that experience. Yet, our need for external validation often keeps us from slowing down and becoming balanced.

I have spent much of my life measuring my importance by the number of things I was doing and the people I was pleasing. I became frustrated when I wasn't participating in the scores of activities life presented. Of course, I just became more and more stressed. Dr. Hans Selye, the great pioneer in the field of stress, said that most emotional stress is caused by trying to be something we are not. I think that fits many of us. In an attempt to earn a sense of value, many of us overperform and overachieve, feeling driven to prove ourselves indispensable to others.

Addiction to human praise throws our life out of balance. Satisfying others at the expense of ourselves throws us out of balance. We become dysfunctional when we get hooked into other people's approval, into mistakenly acting as though self-sacrifice will buy us self-esteem. Saying things day after day that we don't feel and doing things day after day that don't nurture our soul greatly affect our emotional and physical health. Sometimes what is behind our drive is our attempt to make up for what we perceive as defects in us, but with that motive, we do not feel whole regardless of what we accomplish. Pursuing accomplishments to make up for a sense of lack or inferiority only generates additional compulsive behaviors and anxiety.

We can exhaust ourselves striving to meet the expectations of others and trying to satisfy expectations that are unrealistic. This behavior is particularly true of the "perfectionist." For the perfectionists who have so thoroughly trained themselves to constantly "do," just "being" can feel like dissolving into nothingness or ceasing to exist. Perfectionists are driven by the past messages that told them they weren't good enough. Now they are out to prove that not only are they good enough, but they are the best. Though there are times when we want performance perfectionism ("our" surgeon, "our" pilot), perfectionism in general blocks our progress, because it sets an impossible standard and ultimately results in self-criticism and imbalance.

The messengers of anxiety, confusion, and despair painfully remind us that perfectionism doesn't work. They tell us that we need to reassess and readjust. We need to heed this call. Yet, if you have spent your life directing your energy into being perfect or to prove yourself or to justify your existence, intense anxieties can surface when you attempt to redirect that energy into discovering and loving yourself. But stay determined to let your spirit be your reference point rather than following the incessant demands of your wounded self-worth.

It took some time for me to see how much I was taking on in order to compensate for my deeper feelings of inadequacy and inferiority. But as my truth evolved, I slowly began to detach from needing the approval of others and began to create more time for myself by eliminating some of the less fulfilling and more superficial activities which had been requiring my attention. Once I managed to bring more balance into my life, I found I enjoyed more thoroughly those select activities in which I did involve myself, and I was more relaxed and present.

Sharon Wegscheider-Cruse writes in her book *The*

*Miracle of Recovery* about various cycles in which her life became so out of balance and her years of constant searching before slowing down to absorb what she was learning and to heal her pain. Those years of searching took her to classes, conferences, healing centers, and support groups, followed by her immediate return to a demanding schedule of teaching as fast as she was learning. She writes, "So while I was making all the efforts to search and to try to learn and to experience, I literally was wearing myself out and avoiding my continuing pain. I took everything that I had learned and began to give away to others before I began to take for myself." Finally, she realized that the most important thing she needed to do was stop, surrender, heal, and then give whatever she could to those around her.

Many of us can relate to Wegscheider-Cruse's story because we neglect our well-being for the sake of others. Somehow we got the idea that self-nurturing is "selfish." However, if our life revolves around meeting the needs of others, and we rarely have any time for ourselves, except to occasionally collapse, we are not honoring our own worth. It is an act of self-love and self-respect to let our needs matter, to balance our responsibility for taking care of ourselves with our duty to help others. It is also important to remember that everything we do is infused with the energy in which we do it, so being a patient and understanding person when we are always functioning on the edge is difficult.

If you aren't sure if your life has become unbalanced because of your sacrifice to others, take this little quiz. Are you so busy taking care of other people that you don't take care of yourself? Do you find that your own needs often get pushed to the side? Do you feel compelled to listen to every person who wants to tell you a story, ask you a question, or make a comment regardless of your level of fatigue? If you're answering yes to these questions, you need to be as concerned with self-cultivation and your own inner harmony as you are with your relationships with others. When you do a good job taking care of yourself, you are free to be useful to others.

Give yourself permission to do those things that bring you joy and laughter. Give yourself permission to engage in those activities that may not be valued by other people but do address your needs and desires. Maybe a friend tells you that spending your money on massage therapy is too frivolous, so you hesitate or feel guilty. Or maybe your spouse doesn't understand your need for solitude, so you give it up to be accommodating. Give yourself permission to identify and address your own legitimate requirements without needing the approval of others.

The ability to have fun, laugh, and celebrate is crucial to the quality of our life and to maintaining balance. Fun adds joy to our life and allows us to renew our spirit and strength. Fun is taking time to rejoice being alive, and recreation gives us a chance to "re-create" ourselves. How sad to live our days so structured and serious that there is little time for spontaneous play, for taking on different roles, and for lots of laughter. Laughter triggers relief and makes stress and pain more bearable. It also breaks down the walls that separate us from others and ourselves.

I had a big breakthrough in life when my need to play and renew myself became as important as my need to check off everything on my to-do list. I rediscovered the child within me who possesses that sense of wonder. I rediscovered that feeling of participating fully in life. I realized I had been spending my existence running in a panic as though a pack of wolves were after me. I learned I could let go of many things that once seemed urgent and simply play, laugh, and have fun.

Like me, perhaps you need to make a choice to keep work in balanced proportion to play. I encourage you not to make the mistake of spending so much time on doing the right things and getting the work done that there is no time for loving and enjoying life. Don't allow being busy to become a status symbol. Pause to savor success, to spend time with loved ones, to enjoy hobbies, and to rest. Balance your working life with taking the time to stretch your mind in different directions. Play sports and games of all kinds, take classes, develop new hobbies, read books, and engage in other activities that stimulate your creativity. Refuse to let work dominate your life and keep you off balance.

There are many ways we can maintain or restore equilibrium to our body and mind so that our joy and good health can flourish. Incorporating activities such as exercise, massage, meditation, and prayer is enormously beneficial. Exercise not only promotes our health, but it also promotes our self-esteem. When we feel physically vibrant and strong, our confidence grows and our desire to take action in all areas of life increases. Most of the reasons we give for not exercising have to do with time and energy, yet the fastest way to gain energy is to exercise. Unfortunately, when we are stressed, we tend to spend our time doing more of those things that drain energy and less of the things that give us energy.

If jogging or lifting weights or playing a game of basketball isn't the type of exercising you like to do, find something that brings you pleasure. In my early twenties, I signed up for a hatha yoga class at a local YWCA. I was hooked, so in the spring of 1980, I attended my first Yoga Retreat, which was taught by Lilias Folan. I left knowing yoga was a path for me; for it wasn't just about exercise. It was about an integration of my body, mind, and spirit. It was also an introduction to experiencing high energy in a calm state. Prior to yoga, my high energy level was usually coupled with high tension. Yoga taught me to be vibrantly alive while calm and still.

Another means of promoting a calm but alert state of

mind is through massage. Massage not only reduces stress and tension, but it can also help you reach an altered state, a spiritual plane, which facilitates healing. My dear friend Pamela Englebert is a nurse massage therapist. Pamela has taught me much about the powerful healing of touch and its value in returning the body and mind to equilibrium. Under her gentle guidance, I have learned how emotional memory is stored in many places in the body and how massage can unlock these trapped emotions and feelings.

We have so many options for honoring our need for balance. Actually, it is more than a need. It is a necessity. We have only to observe nature to learn much about this essential dynamic of life. As we look around us, we see the rhythms of nature always working to maintain balance, beginning with the cycle of breathing. Humans and other animals breathe oxygen and release carbon dioxide. Plants use carbon dioxide and release oxygen. As long as that balance maintains itself, everything flows perfectly. Nature maintains the balance of the earth's water through a phenomenon known as the hydrologic cycle. This cycle has kept the volume of the earth's water constant for the last three million years. The list is endless as to how nature demonstrates the necessity of balance.

In choosing to honor our need for balance, we contribute to life, for the more balanced we become the more sanity we bring to the world. Moving toward creating more balance in our individual lives allows us to live with even greater integrity, kindness, love, and caring. Wouldn't that be a giant step toward nurturing the greatness within you?

# 5

# Self-Awareness

More than two thousand years ago, the philosopher Plato founded a school in ancient Greece. Above the entrance to that school, a very brief motto was carved in stone: Know Thyself. In every philosophy and self-help program from ancient times to the modern human potential movement, one doctrine has remained unchanged, and that is the call to *know thyself.* The most powerful knowledge you can possess is that which you gain about yourself. Self-knowledge enables you to understand who you really are and why you do the things you do. Self-knowledge empowers you to make choices that serve you.

The Eastern saying, "He who conquers a city is great; he who conquers himself is mighty," is a profound summarization of the power of self-knowledge. Conquering ourselves requires extraordinary strength and self-awareness. This self-awareness is developed through rigorous self-examination and honesty—through learning to listen and watch ourselves and becoming aware of our feelings.

Self-awareness is not just navel-gazing narcissism. It is not about spending an endless amount of time examining personal problems and becoming totally preoccupied with them. It is a lifelong process of understanding what makes you tick as a unique individual. It is understanding who you are and where you want to go.

There is little as utterly fascinating to us as human beings as making sense of our lives. We want to experience meaning in our life; it is our main concern. Therefore, it is of great importance to ask ourselves the questions: Who am I? What is life all about? What is truly worthwhile? Why am I? This inquiring attitude is healthy. These are not eccentric questions at all, but important and worthwhile ones. By staying open to these perhaps unanswerable mysteries of human existence, we can create a rich, meaningful, and authentic life.

The richness of life depends upon finding out who we are. So many of us don't know who we truly are or what we feel. We are numbed out or cut off from our feelings and sleepwalking through life. We seem to be roaming around in a self-induced fog just going through the motions of living.

To understand our wants and needs and to possess a sense of meaning and purpose, we must look inside; we must pay attention to our feelings. The more attention we pay to our inner world, the more familiar we become with it, and the more we learn. We then begin to discover answers to life's most meaningful questions.

Unfortunately, for many of us, we have looked outside ourself for answers. We have based our meaning and sense of security on those things in life that are guaranteed to change and fluctuate. We have reached outward to people, accomplishments, and things to feel important, valuable, safe, and loved. Nevertheless, all of our activities and relationships, pleasurable as they may be, won't satisfy our deepest longings. At the core of our being is a spiritual need that can only be met by turning inward to find our own happiness and to seek our own truth.

The wisest thing we can do is to seek meaning and happiness, not in outside things, but within ourselves, for no external source of achievement or relationship can provide lasting happiness and inner security. In fact, we are sometimes surprised to find that our success in the world doesn't always bring the anticipated sense of fulfillment, and that we are left with a sense of gnawing anxiety and emptiness. But herein lies our opportunity, for as Carl Jung wrote, "Your inner emptiness conceals just as great a fullness if you only allow it."

This is the true hero's journey, traveling within and facing ourselves and allowing our inner emptiness to reveal this great fullness. As we travel within, we find happiness and move forward in the most meaningful sense. For as we go deeper, we gain self-knowledge.

Without self-knowledge, we tend to drift with the tides of life, adapting, coping, and trying to survive as best we can. Without self-knowledge, we live unconsciously—a slave to our unconscious fears and desires. We tune out those things we don't want to deal with and avoid reality, choosing self-avoidance rather than self-confrontation. We hide from the truth about our relationships, the truth about our health habits, the truth about how we really feel about ourselves, and the truth about where our choices are truly leading us.

We pretend not to notice. We pretend not to notice the lack of pleasure in our life, the amount of drinking in which our spouse is indulging, the erratic moods of our child, the unhappiness in our marriage, or the anger in our own voice. Yet deep inside we know something isn't right; we hurt. So we find ways to escape the grief and pain within—drugs, work, television, consumerism, relationships, and on and on. In our attempts to experience some measure of happiness and to alienate ourselves from our distress, we search for something outside of ourselves to heal inside wounds.

As long as we refuse to see the wounds, we will continue to live unconsciously, filling ourselves with a myriad of distractions. We will continue our constant activity, staying on the move to keep our anxiety at bay. We will continue to create what Thoreau called "lives of quiet desperation," lives that are so far from what we initially dreamed, or successes that are more hollow than we could have ever imagined.

Living unconsciously is self-destructive, as avoiding the truth insulates us from the very information we need to learn and grow. Confessing the truth to ourselves is one of the most difficult challenges we face, yet it leads us to our liberation. When we don't face the truth, we continue our negative habits and recycle our drama.

A number of years ago, I worked at Charter Lake Psychiatric Hospital in Macon, Georgia, with Connie Dominy, a therapist affectionately known as "Drill Sergeant." Often Connie would ask a patient, "Why did you do that?" Nine times out of ten, the patient would answer, "I don't know." Connie would look them straight in the eye and say, "Well, let yourself know."

Connie knew healing required living consciously and facing the truth; otherwise, we re-create negative patterns. She understood that old unprocessed hurts are like microchips buried deep inside that are programmed to keep sending out the same fixed messages. She knew that if we don't confront our self-sabotaging patterns, they will run havoc in our life.

I remember working with a manager who struck me as having a self-sabotaging pattern. He appeared to be possessed with the need to "be right." One of his complaints was that his coworkers rarely confided in him and he often felt excluded. He then went on to express that he felt this same way with his wife and children. I inquired as to whether he had ever discussed this with his wife. He said that he indeed had discussed it with her, and she informed him that she rarely talked to him anymore because he never really listened, and he always seemed to have the answer. He continued to explain that he didn't need to listen, because most of the time, he knew what she was going to say before she even "opened her mouth." As our conversation progressed, it appeared that he saw no connection between his behavior and people's avoidance of him.

The process of becoming an aware, conscious person is about waking up to what you are doing, why you're doing it, and the outcome your actions are producing. Becoming aware is about facing what you've created in your life so that you can open the door to changing what isn't working for you and making healthier, more effective choices. Becoming aware is about understanding the motivating force behind your actions and intentions and choosing responsibly. Our awareness of ourselves, our total honesty with ourselves, and our willingness to take responsibility are the foundation of living consciously.

Dr. Phil McGraw's way of describing living consciously is "You either get it, or you don't." In his book *Life Strategies,* McGraw writes, "In almost every situation, there are people who get it and there are people who don't—and it's really easy to tell them apart. Those who get it are enjoying the fruits of their knowledge. Those who don't spend a lot of time looking puzzled, frustrated, and doing without."

The slapstick comedy *National Lampoon's Christmas Vacation* typifies the chaos and catastrophe that can result when we move through the world with little awareness. Cousin Eddie is a particularly good example of someone who clearly doesn't get it. This is so revealing in the scene when Clark is introducing his boss to Cousin Eddie and refers to him as "my cousin-in-law, whose heart is bigger than his brain." At that point, thinking he had just received a compliment, Cousin Eddie humbly responds, "I appreciate that, Clark." With a heart bigger than his brain, Cousin Eddie creates catastrophe after catastrophe.

Just as with the unaware manager and Cousin Eddie, misunderstandings and complications are inevitable when we avoid facing our dysfunctional behavior and approach life with a kind of habitual, automatic, mechanical process of reacting. However, facing our unhealthy conduct and admitting that something in our life isn't working can create such feelings of discomfort that we choose not to deal with the pain of self-reflection. We choose instead to continue with the negative patterns and involve ourselves in immediate gratification over growth. Thus, by trying to avoid pain, we create even more pain. We then move through life experiencing repeatedly the damaging results of our self-destructive patterns.

Becoming conscious allows us the opportunity to end our self-destructive patterns, but doing so involves experiencing emotions we don't want to feel and having new insights into things we would prefer not to see. But to become conscious, we must face the truth. The avoidance of facing the truth and the hurt it might produce only gives it a hiding place from which it ambushes us. The very tip of that infamous iceberg the *Titanic* struck was visible, but the part that wasn't seen was much, much larger. That unseen part did the damage. Trying to hide from our pain and problems, to distract ourselves or to run away from them, is simply a temporary fix. Our problems, when ignored, have a way of turning into bigger problems, even into full-fledged crises.

Many people have become invested in trying to protect themselves from unpleasant emotions. They have anesthetized a huge portion of their feeling self. They are so dissociated from their feelings that they have become highly skilled performers, unconsciously playing out whatever part seems necessary at the moment. Occasionally, they allow themselves to feel their feelings, to experience the spontaneous response of their heart, but they find the intensity of it all so frightening that they close down again. Sadly, by trying to deaden themselves to their pain, they also deaden themselves to joy, for suppressing negative emotions also means suppressing the ability to feel positive emotions.

If we associate expressing our feelings with pain, we are less likely to do it. However, if we understood that *not* expressing our feelings means pain, we might allow ourselves to be more vulnerable. If we clearly understood that unexpressed feelings become distorted, affect our reasoning, build up inside, and make us feel crazy, then we might have more of a willingness to feel them. The irony is that we suppress our feelings out of fear that only creates more fear. If we would allow ourselves to face our fears and to feel the feelings we've been trying to avoid, the pressure and power of those fears would be relieved, and we would discover that our fears really aren't as big as we thought.

By allowing ourselves to experience what we feel without judgment or resistance, and with compassion, we create our path to freedom. Freedom comes as we fully embrace our emotions and breathe into them instead of pushing them away. By doing so, they lose their power over us, and we then have the opportunity to gain the wisdom they offer. As the poet Robert Frost said, "The best way out is always through."

Moving through our feelings often takes us to dark places within. We can think of these dark places as old wounds. Old wounds are like holes that allow our joy to slip away. Many of these old wounds have to do with the pain, grief, and misunderstandings rooted in childhood years. We can try to protect ourselves by blocking out these hurtful memories, but if we don't deal with them, or acknowledge them, they will continue to run us. We need to invite the past into our awareness to understand how it has shaped the present. David Richo writes in *How to Be an Adult,* "What we leave incomplete we are doomed to repeat. The untreated traumas of childhood become the frustrating dramas of adulthood."

Our adult dramas begin to make some sense to us when we understand their origin. For example, the woman who repeatedly chooses the unavailable man may unconsciously be re-creating the drama with her unavailable father. Or the man who repeatedly finds himself in a relationship with a controlling woman may unconsciously be reenacting the entanglement with his controlling mother. Or the workaholic whose life is totally out of balance may be hoping that his achievement will finally win him his father's blessing. The list is endless.

The old wounds and pain that we repress and refuse to acknowledge live in our unconscious mind, generating emotional distress. To protect ourselves from this distress, we unconsciously use defense mechanisms. Our defense mechanisms keep us from feeling overwhelmed by painful or threatening feelings; they are essentially escapes. They also reflect our wounds.

Denial is one of the most preferred mechanisms. It can be a survival strategy for a while, but it is not a way to live; denying our buried emotions and the truth of "what is" keeps us trapped. We don't change those things we deny to be true.

I witnessed an interesting scenario that epitomized denial. It happened with a woman who was describing to me her husband's anger over the fact that she gave away his old golf clubs. She explained she did this in an effort to clean out the garage. During our conversation, she denied any anger toward her husband that might have motivated such an action and was surprised that he would care about "old" golf clubs. Her hurt and resentment seemed very close to the surface to me, but she denied anything but an honest effort to "get things organized."

Like this woman, we often deny or rationalize the obvious because to accept it would mean we would have to do something about it, which scares us half to death. What would it mean to stand up and speak our truth? What would appear to be at stake that we don't want to risk? What changes might it create with which we don't want to deal? Often we know the answers to our questions, but we don't want to hear them. We don't want to change. We might want things to change, but "we" don't want to change. But if we are to live consciously, we must change even though growth can be painful.

Moving forward requires taking action and making decisions that can be distressing and filled with difficult adjustments; therefore, growth can be painful. To dismantle a life that isn't working often feels terrifying, as moving out of our comfort zone, even when it is totally toxic, arouses our hidden fears. Until we are willing to face our fears and to be open to change, we will find ourselves stuck in unhappiness and frustration.

Facing our fears involves facing the truth. Facing the truth often means replacing our fantasy world with the real world of facts and allowing the light of truth to shine upon our actions. As we choose to deal with the truth, we respect ourselves more. Living consciously generates self-respect, self-confidence, and personal power. It also generates wisdom, which is the ability to reflect upon our experiences and to learn from them.

Make it a habit to consciously practice staying in touch with your inner truth and with the truth of what is really happening around you. Make it a habit to be genuine and notice when you are not. Develop the willingness to face your internal feelings and work with them with awareness. Susan Thesenga writes in *The Undefended Self,* "Every fault acknowledged, every defense dismantled, and every pain felt and released, gives us powerful new reserves of thought and feeling for creating our lives in positive new directions. And, on the other hand, every negative attitude unconsciously perpetrated, every defense held onto, and every pain denied, ties up our life energies and limits our consciousness."

Examining our negative attitudes, releasing our defenses, and owning our pain often introduces us to the shadow side of our personality. Healing requires that we confront the shadow side of ourselves, the hidden parts. The shadow refers to everything that has been repressed or denied and embodies all of life that has not been allowed expression. Robert Louis Stevenson's tale of Dr. Jekyll and Mr. Hyde is the symbolic story of a man and his shadow.

In Stevenson's story, Dr. Henry Jekyll's enthusiasm for science and his selfless acts of service made him a much-admired man, but a friend convinced him that he needed to allow his sensual nature more expression. After a visit to a music hall where he watched an alluring dancer, Jekyll became fascinated with the contrasting aspects of human nature and soon obsessed with the idea of separating them. Finally, he creates a potion by which he could transform into Edward Hyde, the physical manifestation of his evil side. He alternates between the two completely different personalities until the evil side eventually takes over.

Though in less dramatic ways, if we don't deal with our evil (shadow) side, we will find it taking over in unexpected and often subtle forms. For example, our shadow side is often revealed through our judgments and criticisms of other people. The people we are most judgmental of are the people most similar to disowned parts of ourselves. We sometimes see this with people deemed to be the most respected and upright members of their church as they lash out with judgmental, cruel, and vindictive behavior toward those perceived as falling short of their moral standards.

Pastor Ted Haggard, former president of the National Association of Evangelicals, condemned gay marriage and consistently presented his wife and five children as a family model. At one point in his Colorado Springs ministry, Haggard focused his efforts on homosexuals by frequenting gay bars and inviting men to his congregation. Yet, it was reported that for years Haggard had been having drug-fueled homosexual trysts. Ted Haggard's shadow side played itself out on the world stage.

These hypocritical scenarios are often the outcome when we vigorously deny our own shadow side and project our denial toward others. Marion Woodman calls projection "an unconscious arrow." Unconsciously, we launch onto others those impulses and traits that we ourselves have but cannot accept. When we do not own or deal with these impulses and traits (our shadow), we are forced to act them out through projection or other means. Our "acting out" will happen, for our repressed parts will reassert themselves. But when we bring to consciousness and expose what we are projecting, we don't have to project it anymore.

One of my most important teachers in my efforts to understand the shadow and how we act it out was Dr. Elisabeth Kubler Ross. Many years ago, I participated in a workshop with Dr. Ross, and I have such a vivid memory of her saying, "We each have our inner Mother Theresa and our inner Hitler." That struck me in such a profound way and led me to explore my own inner Hitler—the part of me that could be mean and cruel to others. It also provoked a deep desire to have my "inner Mother Theresa" dominate more of my personality.

I left that workshop feeling clear that until we examine our shadow side and heal our own wounds, we will wound others. For those of us who have been abused, we become the abusers; we become the wounded now inflicting the wounds unless we interrupt the pattern. And to the extent that we remain unconscious, our children will suffer—the sins of one generation visiting the next.

The good news is that as we face our shadow, heal our wounds, and grow in self-awareness, we begin to find peace within. The peace we find within we bring to the world. Thus, as we evolve individually, the consciousness of the world changes, for we each have an effect on the consciousness of the world.

Some years ago, I attended a World Balance Conference in Snowmass, Colorado, which dealt with transforming the consciousness of the world. Speakers from all disciplines gathered to discuss creating a more conscious, loving, and peaceful planet. One of my favorite presentations was by the late Dennis Weaver. Weaver reminded us that world balance begins with individual balance and what we are inwardly is reflected outwardly. He said, "Utopia must spring in the private bosom."

We create our own utopia as we heal and love ourself. In the process, we become more self-aware, and we realize that by doing so we are making a great contribution to life. We realize that our commitment to self-awareness and its inevitable outcomes is not for us alone, but all of humanity. As Meister Eckhart, a thirteenth-century German mystic stated, "The outward work will never be puny if the inward work is great."

With "inward work," we achieve greater self-awareness, which results in more freedom and more creativity. Self-awareness unlocks creativity in that it gives us a new way of perceiving ourselves, the world, and our possibilities. We, therefore, have a greater realization of our potential. In fact, as we begin to have a deeper understanding of ourselves, we find our creativity and potential exploding in ways that will surprise and delight us. We find ourselves like a diver, descending to the depths of our soul and often returning with a pearl of great price.

# 6

# Integrity

One of America's most famous hero/villains, Benedict Arnold, was a man driven by neediness and little self-awareness. The hunger for attention and power drove this brilliant battlefield general to betray his country and sacrifice his integrity. Benedict Arnold's penchant for danger began early as he learned to survive a difficult childhood by being a brave daredevil, later thriving on the attention his daredevilishness received. His father was an alcoholic who drank himself into a stupor as the family's fortunes raged up and down. Young Benedict coped by becoming more and more outrageous in his behavior. He reached the point where violence and great risks exhilarated him.

He was a person who had few thoughts about being good or bad; he just knew what he wanted and went after it. He lived his life consumed with his own importance and demanded the respect of others without showing respect. Benedict Arnold died a broken man beset by torments. His lack of integrity led to the consequences he most wanted to avoid.

The outcome couldn't have happened otherwise. Trouble awaits when we move through life pumped up with our own sense of self-importance, permitting our neediness and greediness to drive us to dishonorable behavior. Allowing such cravings to toss out our moral judgment is self-defeating and, at the most, offers some instant gratification. Unfortunately, we tend to live based on instant gratification, which often leads to us giving up our personal honor for short-term gain.

Giving up our personal honor is fueled by feelings of

fear and frustration that overwhelm our moral principles. Perhaps we fear the consequences of a failing grade, so we cheat on a test. Perhaps we feel frustrated with our partner, so we commit acts of infidelity. Or maybe we feel inadequate in the eyes of another, so we lie or embellish to make ourselves feel more grandiose. Perhaps we fear the pain of rejection or the pain of loneliness, so we don't stand up and speak our truth for fear of being alienated. Or we involve ourselves in unhealthy relationships that require a sacrifice of our own personal values, so we won't have to deal with the pain of loneliness.

These actions, as well as all the actions we take, are simply attempts to meet our needs. The more needy and deprived we feel, the more apt we are to act immorally. Whether the feelings of deprivation have to do with love, money, attention, respect, power, or something else, a way will be found to meet those needs. Our hurt, frightened self engages in indecent, self-defeating conduct, though our fearful self is typically masked by arrogance. The challenge is to develop a greater self-awareness of our needs, drop the mask, and find the most appropriate ways to get our needs met.

Benedict Arnold used the most destructive and self-defeating ways to get his needs met. Moreover, like Benedict Arnold, all of us have dealt with the struggle between morality and self-interest, with our self-importance wanting to take center stage. These are the times when our selfish impulses conflict with our internal moral compass. Dr. Laura Schlessinger writes in her book *How Could You Do That?!*, "Life is often quite tough, challenging us to choose between seemingly esoteric, intangible ideals and getting goodies or good vibes right now. You have character when you most often choose ideals."

We have all had times when we did not choose our ideals, or when we have done things that did not reflect the best of our character. The important thing is that we keep trying. We must continue striving to take the high road regardless of what stands before us. Abraham Lincoln is often quoted as saying, "I am not bound to win, but I am bound to be true. I am not bound to succeed, but I am bound to live up to the light I have." Committing ourselves to living up to our own light of truth contributes not only to our own life, but to the world. When we live focused and centered in the light of truth and honor, we become a shining beacon.

When we let the most important thing in life be who we are as a person and who we unceasingly endeavor to become, we add great value to the world. Committing to being a person of value and pursuing only what is honorable, what is good, and what is true will result in a deep immeasurable sense of peace and satisfaction.

The truest test of our character arises in our actions, in the practice of our values. In the final analysis, it is what we do that tells others and ourselves what kind of person we are, what our deepest values are. What we do reveals who we are, so we must be rigorous and consistent with our words and actions. Being consistent with our words and actions is being congruent. It is aligning who we are on the inside with how we behave on the outside.

Jeannette Rankin, the first woman elected to the U.S. Congress, faced the challenge of being congruent with her values and acting with integrity concerning her own truth. Rankin felt strongly that war was wrong; she could not see how killing and fighting could ever solve the world's problems. As a result, she voted against U.S. entry into World War I counter to the advice of her own family, close friends, and other congressmen. Her difficult decision to follow her own beliefs was a great act of courage. Though she disappointed many people, she was true to herself.

Rankin's stand against the war was not popular, and she was not reelected for another term until twenty-four years later. Then, once again, Congresswoman Rankin had to decide to vote "yes" or "no" on America's going to war.

For a second time, she voted "no," the only representative to vote against war with Japan. Her closest friends cursed and shunned her. She stood alone. Though many believed Jeannette Rankin turned against her country when it needed her most, she believed she could not turn against her values.

Jeannette Rankin had the courage to follow her inner voice when it meant going against the crowd. She was so driven by her internal principles that she wasn't concerned with what people thought and refused to shift her standards in order to enhance herself in the eyes of others. She allowed her actions to reflect who she was in her heart. She knew that acting from her center was far more potent than being accepted and approved by others.

Sometimes, out of our need for approval and fear of rejection, we pretend to be what we are not. Consequently, we lose touch with our true self and look outward for our meaning and identity, making us vulnerable to compromising our integrity even more. What is needed is to reconnect with our true self and refuse to compromise our integrity by trying to be or say or feel something that is not true for us. We need to honor our authentic self.

We live in a society that neither encourages us to honor our true self nor promotes honesty. In fact, dishonesty is rampant. We have become desensitized to lies through living in a world where spin-doctors operate. Stretching the facts, rationalizing, or leaving out details that may cloud the truth is the function of spinning. Somewhere between the truth and a lie, there's "spin"—filtering news and information through one's agendas to reflect a certain point of view and advocating it as the "truth." Advertisers have their own version of this when they tell us that their product is the absolute best or that we will experience instant relief or a permanent cure. We must remember that ethical speech is about what is said and not said.

Withholding is a form of lying, whether we are withholding the truth from others or ourselves. And cover-ups bother most of us more than the original misdeed, especially when cover-ups are masqueraded as foul-ups, which is often the case in politics. The effort to camouflage, minimize, and deny the truth slowly erodes trust. There is much truth to the old saying, "We can't talk ourselves out of problems we behaved ourselves into." Those buried splinters of truth have a way of working themselves to the surface.

We have watched these splinters of truths emerge in the world of politics, a world where many leaders do not think the rules apply to them, who do not live by the truth that the way they behave is more important than what they've achieved. We have witnessed how brains and ability without integrity are damaging. We've watched disruption occur as individuals who are too morally immature to deal with the power of their position make dreadful choices. Scandals have become so much a part of our society that we begin to wonder if immaturity and weaknesses of character are the norm. Our trust has been steadily declining, and our values are in question. Deepak Chopra writes in his book *Creating Affluence,* "Without values, there is confusion and chaos. When values disintegrate everything disintegrates. Health disintegrates, poverty attains dominance over affluence, societies and civilizations crumble."

The good news is that the crash and scandal of major corporations like Enron, WorldCom, and Arthur Andersen have given us the opportunity to awaken from our moral slumber and rebuild trust by establishing a set of moral imperatives. These public examples so sadly lacking in morals have given us the opportunity to insist that success be achieved at the service of others, not the expense. They have presented us with the possibility of strengthening the values by which we live.

Only when we honor the right kinds of values do we maintain stability and flourish. Focusing on what's important in our lives, as well as identifying and eliminating things that are not honorable and do not help us grow, moves us forward in a positive direction. Our values and beliefs are the driving force behind us and determine the basic direction of our life. What we focus on is based on our values. In fact, our personal values identify us to others and ourselves. In a sense, we are the values we cherish and demonstrate.

Ruth Simmons's parents cherished the values of hard work and authenticity and admonished her to do the same. A great-great-granddaughter of slaves and the twelfth child of sharecroppers raised in the South during a time of bitter segregation, Simmons rose to become the first African American to lead an Ivy League institution. In July of 2001, she became the first woman president of Brown University. In her essay "My Mother's Daughter: Lessons I Learned in Civility and Authenticity," which appeared in *Texas Journal of Ideas, History and Culture* in 1998, Ruth Simmons said, "I was intent on doing something productive and on being everything my parents taught me to be. Their values were clear: do good work; don't ever get too big for your breeches; always be an authentic person; don't worry too much about being famous and rich because that doesn't amount to too much."

Unfortunately, not everyone follows these values, as we often see people so focused on being famous and rich that they abandon a high standard of life for a high standard of living. They become so fixated on attaining material things that they give up their integrity and allow the things of no value to drive from their minds the things of value. They find themselves trading integrity for status or power and being more concerned with being a world-class superstar than a world-class person. They are eager to soak up adulation when their behavior doesn't warrant such admiration. Mark Twain cautioned, "It is better to deserve honors and not have them than to have them and not deserve them."

Whatever our outward show of achievement, if our honors are based on false values, we will soon find ourselves swallowing a bitter pill. False values are those values that do not serve us in finding the true meaning and purpose of life and are often pursued at the expense of others. People of integrity seek opportunities to serve, not use others. When we honestly consider the well-being of others before we decide to profit ourselves, we become truly successful. We violate our conscience by choosing something that would gratify us at the expense of others.

We need to establish a code of conduct for how we treat people everyday. Our code should require that we be kind in our thoughts and actions and refuse to act with mean-spiritedness. Albert Schweitzer wrote, "A man doesn't have to be an angel in order to be a saint." By showing compassion and living with integrity, we can demonstrate saintly behavior.

There is a story about Gen. Ulysses Grant that demonstrates his refusal to act with mean-spiritedness and remarkable exemplification of compassion. It also shows how character can reach for compassion when others are calling for blood. In a very touching moment in history, General Grant revealed his character as he extended mercy to Gen. Robert E. Lee. With his army surrounded, his men weak and exhausted, Lee realized there was little choice but to surrender to General Grant. After a series of notes between the two leaders, they agreed to meet on April 9, 1865, at the house of Wilmer McLean in the village of Appomattox Court House. The meeting lasted approximately two and one-half hours, and at its conclusion, the bloodiest conflict in the nation's history neared its end.

After signing the surrender terms, Lee mounted his horse to ride off to break the news to the brave fellows whom he had so long commanded that they were now prisoners. As he did, Grant saluted him by raising his hat. Under terms of surrender, the horses and personal baggage belonged to the government, but Grant felt that appropriating these things would be an unnecessary humiliation. Therefore, he allowed the vanquished soldiers to keep their horses and the officers to keep their side arms. After the surrender, the Union men commenced in firing a hundred guns in honor of the victory, but Grant immediately ordered it stopped. He noted in his memoirs, "The Confederates were now our prisoners, and we did not want to exult over their downfall."

At that moment of victory, General Grant did not use the Confederate soldiers for his own selfish exultation. He extended to them the respect that he would have wanted to receive. It has often been said that if you want to test a man's character, give him power. Grant passed the test. He understood that success is not about towering above peers and using commanding positions in life to humiliate others.

Integrity is about choosing what is good and merciful in all aspects of life. It is about choosing to treat each other as unique individuals having intrinsic worth—choosing to treat each other as ends, not merely means. When we are so consumed with our own needs and pumped up with our own self-importance, we see and treat other people as objects. We will approach our affairs with private agendas. The desire to serve others will be replaced by our selfishly wanting to exalt ourselves.

When we are motivated by a desire to serve others, we are less prone to act without integrity. Zig Ziglar says in his book *Success for Dummies* that "the measure of a human being isn't the number of servants he or she has, but the number of people he or she serves." And I love his golden rule: "You can have everything in life you want if you will just help enough other people get what they want." A successful person fosters success in other people. A successful person knows that a life of service is the most fulfilling path, for it allows us to get outside of ourselves, outside of our own ego.

Perhaps you have a desire to serve others but often find an extreme contradiction between the values you profess and what you are actually doing in the world. Maybe you feel that the person you are is not really the person you want to be. It is never too late to change. I was in my thirties before I became serious about clarifying my values. Until then, I was just floating from port to port with no clear sense of direction and making most of my choices based upon my neediness. Once I clarified my values, I began making more self-enhancing rather than self-defeating decisions. I grew in self-respect, and my self-esteem was greatly boosted every time I kept my agreements with my self.

By consciously designing the ideals and values to which I desired to be committed, I felt notably better about myself. As Dr. Martin Luther King Jr. declared, "We must stand for something or we will fall for anything." Get clear on that for which you stand and establish goals for yourself that are in alignment with your values. Then starting with the present moment, strive to the best of your ability to live those ideals. Each day of your life, do small things in a great way. Operate with a high standard of accountability to yourself and let your conduct speak for you.

Not consciously choosing and living our values negatively impacts the world, particularly those to whom we are the closest. If our children hear us lecture about the virtues of honesty, and then hear us lie to our neighbors, or if they are punished when they respond in total honesty because they did not say what the grown-ups wanted to hear, they lose their sense of trust. They observe that we do not always practice what we preach, and they do not see us being honest about our feelings. They see us living an inconsistent set of values.

When we profess high standards of integrity, but our choices in daily life don't reveal such, how believable are we? "Do as I say, not as I do" leads to a loss of credibility. We can try to set ourselves up as role models, but unless our life is worthy of emulation, we will be seen as insincere and hypocritical. The greatest teaching we can ever present is our example. In the New Testament, Jesus says, "By their fruits you shall know them."

Children need parents who have a deep sense of personal responsibility for their ethical behavior and live in harmony with their most esteemed values. They need parents who insist upon impeccable integrity and adhere to high standards. They need parents who plant the seeds and model the virtues of integrity, honesty, respect, self-discipline, and responsibility for them.

One of the saddest things regarding the story of former FBI agent Robert Hanssen, who was convicted of spying for the Russians and sentenced to life in prison without the possibility of parole, is the fact that he has six children. Hanssen, who in twenty-two years of espionage received $600,000 in cash and diamonds from Russian spymasters, told the judge before sentencing, "I apologize for my behavior, I am shamed by it. I have opened the door for calumny against my totally innocent wife and children. I have hurt so many deeply." When I read his story, my heart ached for these six innocent children and the heartbreak they must experience.

A collapse of character leads to a chain of heartbreaking events. It behooves us to think seriously before we act without character or conscience. One act of living without integrity can create an endless drama of events. In the words of Eleanor Roosevelt, "Nothing we do ever stands by itself. If it is good, it will serve some good purpose in the future. If it is evil, it may haunt us and handicap our efforts in unimagined ways." The consequences of our choices are inescapable especially to those we may love the most.

Not only do the negative consequences of our choices hurt others, but also we pay a tremendous price in self-respect when we rationalize wrong behavior. We can mask our unseemly behavior with countless excuses, but in the end, we look at ourselves and know we have failed. Living honorably is an act of love to others and ourself. We must demand that we be true to our highest ideals.

Resulting in no qualms of conscience, being true to our highest ideals gives us peace of mind. Speaking before the House Un-American Activities Committee in 1952 during the McCarthy era, playwright Lillian Hellman expressed the celebrated phrase "I can't cut my conscience to fit this year's fashions." Hellman refused to wear a tag around her neck; she was a person no one could buy. She defined and lived according to what she believed to be true, honest, and real about herself. Hellman refused to sacrifice her self-respect.

It often takes tenacity, perseverance, and an unassailable sense of justice to have the moral fiber not to succumb to outside pressure. It takes courage. Courage is not about how you feel; it is about how you act. In the words of Aristotle, "We become brave by doing brave acts." We find that our life expands when we engage in brave acts and shrinks when we sacrifice our ideals.

We must have the courage to speak our truth and the courage to turn the spotlight on our own actions, habits, and beliefs. Knowing ourselves is perhaps the most difficult task any of us face. Yet self-knowledge is essential to integrity. We must honestly face our flaws as well as our assets. We must pay attention to those times we allow our greediness to overcome our sense of decency. We must become aware of those times that we choose expediency over integrity, those times that if it is expedient to be honest, we will be honest. Otherwise, we will choose the more profitable route. We must examine our lives to see if we are following a code of behavior we sincerely believe to be right, to see if we are translating our values into action.

A good example of translating values into action is an account I read about country-music singer Naomi Judd.

As a twenty-two-year-old single mom of two, Judd lived in Los Angeles, which was a strange city to her, particularly since she had only been out of her home state of Kentucky twice. Now she found herself with no money, no job skills, no car, and two babies to support. Forced to find work within walking distance of her home, she landed a job as a receptionist, and regularly sent letters and cards to family and friends back in Kentucky to appease her homesickness.

Judd wrote, "Since I couldn't drive to the post office, I took stamps from our mailroom and left the correct change in an envelope for the office manager. It never occurred to me not to pay for the stamps. But my honesty struck some as odd—so odd that after a few weeks I was called in to see the manager. As I stood nervously before him, he said, 'We're promoting you to secretary.'"

Behaving with integrity paved Judd's way to success. With her integrity in handling the small, everyday tasks of life, she built trust and loyalty, and her integrity shined. George Washington advised, "Labor to keep alive in your breast that little spark of celestial fire called conscience." By putting the money in the envelope, Judd demonstrated that her conscience was alive.

If we keep that little spark of conscience alive, we empower ourselves to act with honesty and thereby build trust with others. Trust is at the base of all effective relationships. In fact, dishonesty is one of the prime reasons for failed relationships. If we do not speak the truth or play fair, trust slips away; then we must employ many rules and other methods of control. When people know that we do speak the truth and play fair, they don't worry about our motives.

Sometimes we don't speak truthfully or play fairly because we are afraid. We are afraid of facing the consequences that telling the truth might bring, so we lie. Lying is a way to avoid taking responsibility, and it can become a habit. When we lie and behave in ways that are against our values, we sabotage our ability to trust ourselves. Deceit takes a terrible toll on our sense of self-respect and the respect we receive from others, leaving us to face the daunting task of rebuilding trust.

Rebuilding trust is a process and begins with a commitment to engage only in actions that support trust. It involves becoming aware of all the ways in which we have failed to live up to the trust and confidence others placed in us. It involves seeing the situation from the other's point of view and apologizing with sincerity after some thought and consideration without offering excuses.

The loss of trust is a painful experience and often involves a lot of hurt, confusion, anger, and sadness. Dealing with these emotions is critical when rebuilding trust. Trust is fostered when there is freedom to address all feelings, whether they are painful, joyous, or uncomfortable. So many of us have been taught to falsify our emotions, thus the constant pretense alienates us from our true feelings and makes it more difficult to connect and heal.

Summon the courage to connect to your feelings and feel your truth. With compassion and mercy, look at the choices you have made in your life. Try to do this without rejecting yourself or judging yourself harshly, for doing so only sets you up to engage in behaviors that further rob you of a sense of integrity. Offering yourself compassion is exceedingly important, as ultimately it is our harsh self-judgment and lack of self-acceptance that leads to behavior devoid of integrity.

Offer yourself compassion, recognizing that in all of us there is lightness and darkness, greatness and smallness. The Chinese philosopher Mencius said, "Those who follow the part of themselves that is great will become great. Those that follow the part that is small will become small." Be encouraged knowing that you can choose to exemplify the greatness.

# 7

# Self-Worth

Christina Onassis, daughter of the famous Greek tycoon, Aristotle Onassis, was born into a life of ostentatious privilege. Upon her father's death, Onassis inherited billions of dollars in addition to fleets of ships and airplanes, lakes and islands, real estate and large bank accounts. Yet she was so insecure and unsure of herself that she paid friends to be her companions. Onassis's favorite companion was a famous polo player whom she reportedly paid $30,000 a month to be at her beck and call. Sadly, the player played the role while bringing along his young girlfriend. A life that was smacking of the ingredients of a fairy tale was more like a nightmare.

Just before her fourth marriage, a pressman asked her if she was the richest woman in the world, and her frank reply was "Yes, I am the richest woman but the unhappiest." Right after her fourth divorce, another journalist reported Onassis as saying, "I never learned how to find happiness in just being with me." She filled the void in herself with relationships and jet-setting. She was constantly on the go until in her late thirties when she was found dead at a country club in Argentina. Her cause of death, which was reported as suicide, was officially recorded as pulmonary edema.

As Christina Onassis's story reveals, you can be one of the richest and most famous people in the world, but unless you love yourself and feel worthy, none of it really matters. None of it really matters because when you are lacking in self-worth and self-love, you have a gnawing emptiness inside, and you feel cut off from the joy of life. Accompanying that feeling of emptiness is an almost constant feeling of stress, regardless of what you possess or what you accomplish.

This stress comes from self-doubt, which creates a continual need to push and fret in the pursuit of the next thing or the next activity that holds the promise of bringing happiness and a sense of being good enough. The hope is that the next, more perfect person, more expensive car, more luxurious vacation, or fancier home will do what all the other people, cars, vacations, and homes have not been able to do. The problem is that if you don't feel a sense of worthiness within yourself, there's no amount of anything that is enough.

External factors can give us ego strength, but they cannot give us the lasting joy and peace of mind that self-worth brings. They are temporary gifts to be enjoyed or celebrated, but they do not define or dictate our worth. Countless energy invested in unconsciously trying to heal our self-worth with external accomplishments and possessions is a futile path, for a life devoted to consumerism and climbing the social ladder cannot make any lasting difference in the emptiness we feel inside. In fact, it may only aggravate that sense of emptiness. This emptiness and loneliness will remain until we begin to love and value ourselves and come to know our inherent worth. Our worth is intrinsic to us as human beings, and it is a constant, not a variable. We can't lose it, but we can lose sight of it.

We lose sight of our worth in a myriad of ways. Losing this sense of worth often begins early in life when we receive messages from our environment, both directly and indirectly, that our worth is based largely on our accomplishments and what others think. If we were taught to be people-pleasers and constantly concern ourselves with "what the neighbors might think," we were led to believe that other people's opinions of us are more important than our own.

As a child, of course, our parents' opinion was the most important to us. In fact, our entire life centered on our parents and how they saw us. Resisting the ideas that our parents had about us was beyond our scope as young children. If they saw us as difficult, unlovable, or not good enough, we tended to see ourselves in the same way. If they ignored or minimized our needs, we tended to believe our needs were not legitimate or that we weren't worthy or deserving enough to have our needs met.

There is a common fantasy some of us grew up with involving the idea that if we were really good and perfect enough, our parents would love us and would not reject or abandon us. Coming to this conclusion is not surprising since we were often given approval when we performed well and love was withheld when we didn't. Or we were rejected if we had feelings and thoughts that were not in accordance with how our parents wanted us to think and feel. This rejecting and withdrawing behavior gave us the message that acceptance and love are conditional. It fueled our people-pleasing behavior in hopes of warding off the painful feelings of rejection.

To protect ourselves, we frequently became silent, so we wouldn't be shamed for saying or doing anything our parents might not agree with. Thus, we only let the world know that part of us we thought they would approve of, and the rest we hid away. In this process, we abandoned our authenticity, our gifts, our talents, and ourselves. Many of us decided somewhere along the way that it was not okay to be who we really are. As a result, we often found ourselves walking around in a trance unaware of our needs. Sadly, we were socialized to fit in rather than find out who we are.

Most damaging of all is growing up believing that our parents, or a parent, do not love us. This makes it very difficult for us to love ourselves. If our parents don't love us, we feel flawed, and our sense of worth is greatly diminished. We do not see our parents as deficient in their capacity to love; we see ourselves as unlovable. Nevertheless, we are always plotting and planning how we might get the love we need, and this keeps us on the treadmill of seeking "out there" what we must find within.

Many of us were raised by parents deficient in their capacity to love and who exhibited an appalling lack of impulse control. We never knew when the shoe would fall, so we walked on eggshells. In an instant, we could be the victim of a temper tantrum or the witness to a hostile drama. We could suddenly find ourselves being verbally and/or physically abused or emotionally neglected, and we were left feeling that we were not okay.

Our parents were wounded souls whose behavior was simply a repetition of what they had experienced and learned as children. Few were motivated by destructive intentions; their dysfunction was virtually inherited. As Deepak Chopra writes in his book, *Unconditional Life,* "Broken spirits do not see anything wrong in breaking the spirits of their children."

These broken spirits often broke our spirits through their unrelenting criticism. Unfortunately, we absorbed into our own minds the critical attitudes of our parents and learned to parent ourselves the way we were parented. Our capacity for criticism of our own behavior was shaped by the impact of our parents' criticism of us. If we were shamed through harsh ridicule, humiliation, or other negative behaviors, we carry deep wounds that cause us to feel worthless. Until these wounds are healed, our shamed inner core tries to hide it with defensive layers, and we travel through life hypnotized by thoughts of inferiority. In fact, that is what shame is, a feeling of being worthless and not as good as other people. Shame is crippling and creates terrible misery.

Shame can also be created when families insist on keeping secrets. As children, we may have sensed that something abnormal was happening in our family, but our parents assured us nothing was wrong. We may not have been allowed to talk about the reality of the situation, mandated to keep a shroud of silence while family members continued their addictive behaviors, such as alcoholism, sexual abuse, or drug addiction. Thus, our perception of reality was invalidated, and we came to believe that our feelings couldn't be trusted. When our feelings were invalidated and we believed our perceptions were wrong, we often felt shameful for "seeing what we saw."

Unfortunately, it wasn't only in our home environment that we were often shamed or diminished. Sometimes it was in school, where teachers and classmates often tried to reduce their feelings of unworthiness by increasing ours. Perhaps we were victims of bullying or other forms of verbal abuse, or victims of cliques that were exclusionary and cruel. Sometimes it was actually in our church that we were taught that we were born without innate goodness and messages of our unworthiness were pounded into our head. We constantly heard how we "didn't measure up," and that began to color everything we believed about ourselves.

As we grew up, the situation was complicated by the media's encouragement of us having unrealistic expectations of life and ourselves. Most of us weren't mature enough to realize that much of what was presented to us was hype and had very little to do with reality. This cultural propaganda often created feelings of not being good enough regardless of how much we accomplished or possessed, guaranteeing a further drop in our self-worth.

We also weren't mature enough to realize that though certain people do stand out because of their wealth, occupation, talent, social standing, and other artificial standards, this doesn't mean they possess a sense of self-worth. In a famous television interview in which the late

Princess Diana informed the public of her secret disease of bulimia, she stated, "You inflict it upon yourself because your self-esteem is at low ebb, and you don't think you're worthy or valuable." Princess Diana revealed to us that no matter who you are or what you have, you are not immune to the pain of low self-worth.

The good news is that you can learn to value and love yourself and experience yourself as worthy. Moving from a negative, limited sense of yourself to a deeply positive sense is totally within your power. However, you have to be deeply committed to accepting greater ideas about who you are and willing to release your limiting beliefs. When you begin to believe in yourself and to love yourself, you will see things differently, and nothing will be quite the same anymore. I can tell you this with conviction because of my own experience with healing my self-worth.

Though most of my life I presented to the world a bold personality, underneath was a frightened and insecure core. Feelings of unworthiness permeated my being. However, I covered up these feelings of unworthiness and fear with a false bravado. It took years of hard work before I finally gave myself permission to claim my worthiness and to stop being in such an adversarial relationship with myself. Learning to love myself was the breakthrough that made every area of my life better. I found that when I truly began loving, accepting, and approving of myself, things in my life started working.

I learned that what we think about ourself determines what we are and crucially affects every part of our experience. In fact, we see the world through our self-concept. With this understanding, it would seem strange that some people think it is promoting selfishness to encourage people to love themselves. These people confuse genuine self-love with narcissism.

Narcissism is self-centeredness, a type of pseudo-self-love in which a lack of an internal sense of self-worth exists. Narcissistic people tend to be infatuated and obsessed with their own desires to the exclusion, and often to the detriment, of others. They tend to have an unyielding pursuit of their own immediate gratification and become egocentric, developing all kinds of dishonest defense mechanisms as a way of distancing themselves from unpleasant emotions. Of course, their defense mechanisms are counterproductive and actually betray any underlying sense of self-worth.

Learning to love and value ourselves is definitely not an act of selfishness. However, if we are not used to caring for ourselves, we naturally feel uncomfortable and worry about being selfish when we finally do take a stand for our own personal rights and self-care. These feelings do not mean that our new behaviors actually are selfish; it's just that we are so unaccustomed to giving ourselves any priority, and now we have moved out of our comfort zone. People who like and value themselves practice taking a stand for their rights and allow themselves to speak their truth and take care of their needs.

As we begin the process of learning to love, value, and accept ourselves, and to meet our own needs, we become more emotionally healthy and less needy. As our value is internalized, we stop desperately seeking the approval of others, and we are better able to really love and to be there for others. By loving ourselves properly, we are able to love our neighbor and follow that great commandment of religion.

The truth is that we can't love and accept each other until we love and accept ourselves, for the capacity to love others depends on the capacity to love ourselves. All the love we give to the world stems from the love and acceptance we have for ourselves. When we love who we are, we will love our neighbor and we will not hurt ourselves or anyone else. When we stop fighting internally, we stop fighting externally. It is through full acceptance of our own self that we stop the battles within and relax into loving others and ourselves. We also find that people love and accept us when we love and accept ourselves.

When we don't love ourselves, it is easy for others to make us feel inadequate, for our own low self-worth distorts perceptions of what is coming to us from the outside. We take the way we feel about ourselves and project that feeling onto others, and unconsciously create situations in which we are offered ample support for our negative self-views. We also have a tendency to expect rejection, often distrusting expressions of love and support. We then find ourselves moving through life struggling with our relationships and rarely experiencing the love and success we desire.

To have the love and success we desire, we must grow in our ability to experience our value and find our inner beauty. As we grow and evolve in our ability to experience the beauty and love within ourself, we then feel it in the world. This ability to value one's self is developed one choice at a time.

The first choice is to establish the intention to regard yourself as worthy and deserving and engage only in behaviors that will support that intention. The more you engage in behaviors that make you feel proud and are consistent with your professed values, beliefs, and standards, the more positive you will feel about yourself and your self-worth will increase.

To know your values, beliefs, and standards, you must find your own truth—your authentic self. As you discover who you truly are, you must then be you with all your heart and soul. You must make a conscious decision to let your authentic self be stronger than your false self. Do this and your self-respect will increase by leaps and bounds. When you summon your courage and speak out for who you truly are and for what you think is right, you escalate your self-worth.

As you discover your truth and take a stand for your true self, focus on your strengths rather than your weaknesses. Your feelings of worth grow when you center on your successes instead of your so-called failures, when you notice what you do right and acknowledge yourself for that. Unfortunately, we have been conditioned to focus our energies on fixing weaknesses while ignoring strengths. This sets us up to be more focused on what is wrong with us rather than what is right.

Being more aware of what is wrong than what is right has certainly been true for me. Whenever I heard the expression "You must accept yourself," I assumed that meant accepting all that was wrong with me. It never occurred to me that it might mean accepting all that is right. In her book *Kitchen Table Wisdom*, Rachel Naomi Remen talks about those little pictures that often appear in the newspapers over the caption "What's wrong with this picture?" If you looked at the picture carefully, you would see that the table only had three legs or the house had no door. As a child, Nemen says, these pictures would evoke such an "Aha!" for her, but later in her life, she wondered why anyone would want to take such satisfaction in seeing what is missing, what is wrong, what is "broken." Upon reading this, it immediately occurred to me that this is how I had always approached myself: "What's wrong with me? What is missing?"

Many of us become caught in the trap that tells us when we fix all the things that are wrong with us, then we can love ourselves. We postpone happiness and living because we are not who we want to be. We must realize that we do not grow by deploring what we cannot be, but by finding joy in being who we are and in accepting ourselves. Unfortunately, there is little in social conditioning that teaches us self-acceptance, so we must make the choice to give ourselves rock solid self-acceptance.

Even if you want to change something about yourself,

choose to love yourself while working on it. This approach reduces self-criticism and self-bashing. Criticizing ourselves is a self-inflicted burden that causes great suffering and diminishes us in our own mind. Chronic self-criticism keeps us stuck, erodes our confidence, and maintains our body in a state of stress. Continually judging ourselves without mercy keeps us filled with tension.

Become a witness to your inner dialogue and notice if your inner judge is victimizing you. Stop tolerating the abusive voices within. Develop a stubborn refusal to abandon yourself no matter what comes your way. You must learn how to say "no" to anything within yourself that speaks ill of who you are. You have to stop beating your spirit with criticism and replace it with compassion. Compassion is love with wisdom. Compassion is having the courage to embrace your humanness.

I had a wonderful teacher, Dr. Kay Shurden, who worked diligently with me on developing compassion for myself. The self-hate had me so wrapped up in blame and disgust that I found offering compassion to myself enormously difficult. I was always so aggressive when confronting myself. Dr. Shurden wanted me to understand that the essence of self-worth is compassion for one's self; when we have compassion for ourselves, we understand and accept ourselves. Acceptance means neither approving nor disapproving, just simply acceptance. It is an acknowledgment of the facts without value judgments.

Acceptance and compassion does not mean falling prey to pity. Too often, we get caught up in pity for ourselves rather than compassion. With pity, we still see ourselves as victims of this or that, as people who are helpless and out of control. We can step aside from our pity and melodrama; we don't have to stay "stuck." We can compassionately say, "Yes, all of that happened to me, and I have believed all of this negativity about myself. But now I intend to create something wonderful." The possibilities for our life are endless when we step outside the melodrama.

Focusing on what we can create with our life, rather than what went or feels wrong, can empower us to establish and consistently engage in accomplishing worthy goals. It is a huge boost to our self-worth to clarify and accomplish goals that inspire us; goals that come from a place of wanting to create, contribute, and learn; goals which not only help ourselves but others as well. We are less susceptible to feelings of low self-worth when we have inspiring and worthy goals that give us a sense of meaning and purpose.

In pursuing our goals, we need to be aware that our level of self-worth shows up in how we approach achievement. In fact, many in the field of psychology consider an individual's sense of self-worth to be the most important single factor in understanding human performance. If our self-worth is low, we typically find ourselves at one of the extremes of achievement. Either we are so afraid that we "underachieve," or we feel continuously driven to "overachieve."

Both approaches have their roots in fear. With underachieving, the fear of failure is so great that we feel too vulnerable to try new things. Underachievers see making a mistake as an indication of some deficit within, and thus avoid risking the humiliating emotions of failure. As overachievers, we tend to stay busy, which allows us to neglect dealing with our real issues and permits the illusion that we will finally feel good about ourselves with the next accomplishment. Hence, the quest for success can actually be a quest for a sense of worthiness sought through the pursuit of wealth, possessions, and image.

The ideal is to strive for achievement to enhance the enjoyment of our life and to express our creativity, not to prove our worth. Achieving to receive the recognition we hope will prove our worthiness only gives us a temporary feeling of well-being after that success is achieved. We then feel immediately compelled to seek another triumph that will bring more validation.

*Feeling* our worth independent of any of our successes—knowing that our worth is intrinsic to us as human beings and that our successes are just frosting on the cake—is the only sane way to live. Giving ourselves the love, approval, and acceptance that we are so desperately seeking "out there" is the pathway to joy and freedom. The truth is that regardless of all of our "outward" searching, what we are truly longing to experience is the feeling from within of being good enough.

If we didn't judge ourselves so harshly, we might feel good enough. However, some personality types never feel good. The perfectionist personality is a harsh self-critic who often assumes that other people will judge them just as badly for being less than perfect. They have rigid, moralistic judgments of themselves and a constant sense of dissatisfaction regardless of their performance or achievement. They refuse to accept themselves as a human being who can fail and be weak.

Perfectionists are typically "image" conscious and exhaust themselves trying to manage the impression others have of them. They put themselves through all kinds of stress by obsessively protecting their "image," operating from the fear of what they imagine people would think if the *truth* about them were known. Perfectionists focus on maintaining a public self that doesn't necessarily square up with the truth of their private world.

Perfectionism is a painful way to live and is actually a defense mechanism that functions to protect a vulnerable and weak self-image and prevent rejection by "being perfect." Perfectionism, as well as other defense mechanisms, is the way we unconsciously intend to ameliorate anxiety, a short-term relief from painful feelings. Defense mechanisms are psychological strategies we use to cope with reality and to keep our self-image intact. Some mechanisms are useful in helping us to meet life's demands, such as using humor to deal with a painful situation. But when our defenses are used in a rigid, inflexible, and distorted manner, they are unhealthy and detrimental to our well-being.

If we allow ourselves to look at our unhealthy defense mechanisms with a compassionate desire to understand them, we open the door to self-awareness, which is critical to loving and accepting ourselves. This requires that we become a committed observer of our behavior, which is not an easy task, for the very nature of defense mechanisms is that they keep us in denial.

I recall a woman describing how every Christmas she decorated her house from one end to the other and felt absolutely no joy in doing so. Her husband commented that not only did she decorate every room, but also it all had to be perfect. Even the Christmas tree had to be perfect. He added that the entire family had begun to dread her yearly ordeal. I asked why she continued to do this when it lacked joy and was stressful for everyone. Her immediate reply was that her family would be disappointed whether they admitted it or not. She proceeded to defend the whole process. Fortunately, she was willing to pursue the matter a little deeper, and after much reflection, she concluded that she was compelled to do what she thought was "expected" and was concerned for her self-image if she did not.

This woman's increased self-awareness allowed her to see her attachment to the approval of others that made it difficult for her to let go of old behaviors even though they no longer served her. Her liberation could have begun if she had been willing to make the courageous choice to step forward and be her true self no matter how she thought it might appear to others.

We must release the need to look good in the eyes of

others to find freedom to live a life we love. As we do so, we will notice that the more authentic we choose to be, the more powerful we will feel. I once read a story about the great artist Rembrandt that really spoke to me about the value of giving up our attachment to other people's opinions. Rembrandt's wife, Saskia, had been sick for a long time, and while he was painting *The Night Watch*, she died. Rembrandt became grief-stricken. When he learned that the soldiers who were depicted in the work were unhappy with his painting, he became even sadder. (The soldiers, members of the Kloveniers, were reportedly angry because they all wanted to be the same size in the portrait.) Despite his grief and disappointment, Rembrandt kept on painting. In the process, he decided that he didn't care what people thought of his work. As a result, his paintings got even better.

If you, like Rembrandt, no longer wish to continue trying to conform to other people's ideas of who and what you should be, then start with a commitment to truly love and value yourself. Be willing to give up your need for the approval of others, and you will be amazed at how your life gets better.

At the same time, give yourself permission to surround yourself with competent, caring people who will support, nurture, and accept you just as you are. Refuse to align yourself with people who are unavailable and unsupportive. Stop trying to save a relationship or family system at the expense of your own emotional and physical well-being. As you continue on your path of self-awareness and commitment to become more and more your authentic self, you must be willing to let go of old unhealthy relationships that keep you stuck.

Letting go of old unhealthy relationships can cause us to feel guilty and anxious and activate our old need for approval. Letting go of relationships is not about putting people out of our heart, but recognizing the need to limit our interaction and to maintain our boundaries. Begin to understand that creating new relationships with people who share our interest in self-awareness and personal growth is an act of self-love.

Most importantly, choose to honor yourself as a valuable and important being. Think only the highest thoughts about yourself, and choose to love yourself unconditionally. Have the courage to genuinely care and love yourself more each day. Choose to be a loving parent to yourself and give yourself the nurturing and support you need. As you change internally, your life will change externally.

Learning to love yourself can be an exciting and enormously rewarding adventure. Even if you don't know how to love yourself, just be willing. Just know that it is entirely possible to develop a new self-image of worthiness, a feeling of wholeness. As you begin to feel better about yourself, your contribution to humanity becomes even greater, and you increasingly become a powerful force of love, goodness, and healing in the world.

8

# Thoughts

Roger Crawford could have easily focused on how things couldn't be done. Born with birth defects, including a missing foot and misshaped hands, he has become a three-time Hall of Fame recipient. As one of the most accomplished physically challenged athletes, he has won NCAA tennis championships and continues to achieve success in many other fields, including being a highly acclaimed professional speaker and the author of *How High Can You Bounce?* Crawford models for us the truth that we can get whatever we focus on. He chose to focus on the possibilities rather than his handicaps, and his success and opportunities have soared.

Like Roger Crawford, there is little we cannot accomplish if we manage our thinking. If we are willing to do the mental work, we can make incredible positive changes in our life, for we are like magnets attracting to us that which we are thinking and feeling. I once saw a card that read, "If you want to live in a beautiful world, [m]ake your head a beautiful place." What a great way of saying that whatever we are thinking on an ongoing basis we are drawing into our life. We inevitably attract into our life the people and successes that are in harmony with our dominant thoughts. We can be certain that the things occupying our mind will soon be a part of our life, if they are not already.

Countless thoughts are constantly popping into our mind, but we get to select the thoughts upon which we will dwell. We can consciously choose to focus our thoughts only on those things and experiences we want, only on those things that make us feel good. By this deliberate intent, we send our thoughts in this positive direction.

Many years ago while participating in a weeklong Louise Hay Teacher Training Program in San Diego, I had an experience that illustrated just how powerful a redirecting of thought can be on an emotional level. While there, my ex-husband was home packing for a move to another state and would be gone by my return. We were separating. My mind was filled with sad, anxious, and angry thoughts. One morning, when my emotions were particularly intense and we were about to begin our training, Dr. Patricia Crane laid a set of affirmation cards on the table and told us to feel free to take one. I closed my eyes, reached out, and trusted that I would select just the right card for me. I opened my eyes and saw these words: "I am safe; it's only change." Then I turned the card over and read, "I cross all bridges with joy and ease. The 'old' unfolds into wonderful new experiences. My life gets better all the time."

I immediately experienced a dramatic shift in my feeling state. I felt more hopeful, more trusting, and more empowered to handle what lay ahead. As I felt myself let out a deep sigh and relax, I experienced once again how a change in thinking can make all the difference in the world. As Louise Hay says, "It's only a thought, and a thought can be changed. Feelings are thoughts in motion in the body. We have a thought and we get a feeling."

I was reminded in that moment of how our thoughts can make us weak or strong, of how our emotions reflect our thought patterns. I realized how finding ourselves at the mercy of our emotions leaves us feeling anxious and out of control, and how we lose our personal power when our emotional reactions have authority in our life. Our negative emotions are a telltale sign that we are dwelling on thoughts that do not serve us, thoughts that deplete our energy. The lesson is to learn to discipline and direct our thinking, to realize that emotional self-management is a necessity for our success.

A man who is a master at demonstrating emotional self-management is W. Mitchell. His book *The Man Who Would Not Be Defeated* is one of the most inspirational stories I have ever read. W. Mitchell has faced some of life's most insurmountable challenges, yet he has not only survived, but thrived against incredible odds. After a fiery motorcycle accident left him burned over sixty-five percent of his body, and then a few years later an airplane crash left him paralyzed, he continued to prosper and to be victorious in both his professional and personal life. Confined to a wheelchair with a scarred face and fingerless paws, he became mayor of Crested Butte, Colorado, established several businesses, and continued on to develop a very successful career as a professional speaker.

Mitchell says, "Before I was paralyzed there were 10,000 things I could do; now there are 9,000. I can either dwell on the 1,000 I've lost or focus on the 9,000 I have left." He brilliantly models that the only thing that determines whether or not we will be happy or joyful is our ability to manage ourselves emotionally. Despite all the tragedies and horrors of what happened to him, he decided how he was going to think about it and what he planned to do about it.

Unlike W. Mitchell, we may have a perfect body, and we may even have all the worldly treasures life has to offer, but we won't have happiness and true success if we don't think constructively. It is learning to master our emotional states by thinking affirmatively that enables us to live a happier life and empowers us to achieve the things we truly desire. If we don't manage our emotional states, it can cost us virtually everything we want in our life.

Managing your emotional state begins with making a connection with the way you are feeling and your thoughts. Whenever you feel negative emotion, recognize that you are thinking negative thoughts. Then begin to observe your thoughts and make wise choices as to how much energy you will continue to give to your negative thinking. Realize that the old grooves of your thinking run deep and that you have been locked in the prison of your conditioning for a long time, so you must choose to be patient as you undertake the formidable task of changing your mind patterns. For most of us, rather than using our mind, our mind has been using us with its incessant, demanding thinking. Reversing this pattern takes time, perseverance, and openness to new ideas. Otherwise, we will end up living our life as though we prefer to be in a cage.

I lived much of my life as though I preferred to be in a cage with my stubborn resistance to the idea that my own thinking created my negative emotions. For years, I continued with a litany of excuses as to why I often seemed to be in emotional distress. I had no problem justifying my malaise, and when I really wanted to wallow in self-pity, I could easily find some popular song that would glorify my emotional pain. Then I could really get into wailing out this tune and wallowing in my suffering. I didn't question this agony; I thought it was just a necessary part of life. Until one day . . . I was driving along the interstate on a beautiful fall day with LeAnn Rimes blasting from my radio "How Do I Live Without You." As I was singing to the top of my voice, I suddenly thought, "Now this is a pretty pathetic way to think."

Nevertheless, that was only one lucid moment, and unfortunately, much of my thinking continued to be so negative and dysfunctional that it drained my energy. If I didn't get a certain job or contract, then I felt I had every reason to be scared and miserable. If disappointments or challenges came my way (which they inevitably did), that would be my excuse for feeling victimized and full of self-pity. If someone didn't respond to me the way I desired, they were the reason I felt stressed. I blamed other people for making me feel bad, and the result was that I only felt more vulnerable and defenseless.

It took some time for me to accept that the quality of my life is made up of my reactions, and my reactions are determined by my thinking. When I finally began to gain a little clarity about this, I made the commitment to involve myself in the kind of thinking that supported my idea of a happy and fulfilling life and would increase my positive reactions. I committed to directing my thoughts to focus on positive images and to thinking about those things that made me feel good. For example, when someone didn't respond to me the way I desired, I realized I had the option of not taking it personally and refusing to dwell on my disappointment. Accordingly, I gradually began to focus more and more on choosing my own response of love and compassion. Another example would be that when I felt lonely, I would focus on the love I wanted to offer everyone around me and the love that was already present in my life. With practice, I began to develop the habit of thinking about and seeing what I wanted to experience.

In the process of committing to focus on the positives I desired, I began to recognize how much of my emotional responses were habits. I also began to meet the incredible amount of resistance I had in letting go of my negative patterns. My resistance led to questioning whether it was even possible to live a life free of limited thinking, that perhaps even the idea was a pipedream. Yet I continued to challenge myself to release the negative thinking that was in the way of my experiencing a more joyful life and that prevented me from discovering my potential. I committed to using my thoughts to build images of a more successful life and to becoming involved in greater ideas so that greater things would evolve.

It continues to take much practice to reprogram the kinds of thoughts I tend to dwell upon. Everyday I pursue my freedom from the thinking habits of a lifetime. I continue to work at putting order, direction, and harmony in my thoughts. Slowly, I have noticed that thinking in a productive way is becoming more and more a matter of habit. I find that using affirmations helps me to accept new ideas and replace the old ones. I am learning that when I tell my mind what to do—strongly enough, often enough and clearly enough—I see positive results. I am learning to use my thoughts as the tool that they are.

While attending a retreat at the Option Institute in Massachusetts, I had the wonderful opportunity to meet Barry Neil Kaufman, who spoke about the importance of putting order and direction to our thoughts. He talked of a turning point in his life when he decided his life would revolve around three things: (1) being happy, (2) loving as much as he possibly could, and (3) walking next to God. He then chose the belief systems and thoughts that supported this way of living and let go of those that did not. He consciously decided that no matter what was thrown at him, he would respond with love. Kaufman's decision not only impacted his life for good, but his commitment to share what he has learned with others has transformed thousands of lives.

Since returning from the Option Institute, I often find myself using Kaufman's model and asking myself certain questions about my thoughts: Does this thought bring me happiness? Is it a loving thought? Does it help me feel closer to God? Often I have a vigorous struggle quieting my stressful thoughts, but if I compassionately stay with the process, I can calm myself and open my heart to love and joy. I also find that if I begin focusing on what I want rather than what I don't want, my thoughts and feelings automatically change. I notice that my focus determines the way I feel.

A powerful example of how our thoughts affect our feelings was demonstrated in the 1920s through the pioneering work of Dr. Émile Coué. Dr. Coué was a French pharmacist who coined the affirmation "Day by day in every way, I am getting better and better." Dr. Coué formulated this affirmation and offered it as a technique of autosuggestion when he dispensed medicine to people. He taught his patients to repeat this affirmation for two minutes each morning and evening. Using the affirmation alone, the results were dramatic. Then with some patients, in addition to the affirmation, when Dr. Coué gave the medication, he would praise the effectiveness of it. With others, he would say nothing. He found that those who bought the medicine with the added praises of its effectiveness did much better than others using the same medication but with no reassurance of its effectiveness.

Dr. Coué believed that by using affirmations to change one's mental pictures, one could rapidly change the subconscious and, consequently, the body that houses it. He understood that our conscious mind initiates thought, and our subconscious mind translates that thought into reality. Our conscious mind is like the captain of a ship, and our subconscious mind is like the ship. The captain gives the directions, and the subconscious follows.

Athletes have long known the value of working with the subconscious mind through mental pictures and affirmations as they preplay and replay high performance achievement, while telling themselves repeatedly that they are winners. They talk themselves into wins. The success of an athlete is just as dependent on the frequency, intensity, and duration of their mental training program as their physical program. We've all seen how the most talented, strongest, and fastest athletes are not always the ones who win. The ones who win are the ones who win mentally.

Winning mentally does not allow for negative thinking. When you think negatively, you create a negative emotional state, thereby perpetuating more negativity.

Strangely, the typical reaction to a difficult situation is to try to defend or hang on to negative feelings, which really complicate matters. Rather than defend your negative emotions, think of them as warning bells, letting you know that your thoughts are not in harmony with what you truly want. Let them be a warning that you are focusing on things you do not want instead of the things you do want.

As you intentionally shift your focus to what you want, the negative emotions will subside and positive emotions will flow in. This shifting of focus to what you desire and bringing yourself to a state of feeling good is necessary before you can attract what you desire. It is difficult to attract money when you are feeling poor, to attract love when you feel unlovable, to attract health when you are sick, or to attract winning when you feel like a loser. You must put your attention behind life-affirming, positive ideas for whatever you put your attention on grows stronger in your life, and whatever you withdraw your attention from grows weaker.

Many successful people could have easily focused on those things that could have blocked their success. Arnold Schwarzenegger is certainly a good example. Hollywood did not think Schwarzenegger's long difficult name, his strange accent, or highly developed physique would draw filmgoers, but Schwarzenegger had a different idea. Danny DeVito is another example of a person not allowing his early discouraging experiences with the film industry to destroy his dream. He also did not allow his diminutive, chunky stature or balding head to prevent him from becoming one of Hollywood's most successful actors and producers. Like Schwarzenegger, he chose to think those thoughts and maintain those beliefs that empowered him and supported his dreams.

We may have an entirely different set of values from DeVito and Schwarzenegger, but like them, we can choose to select thoughts and feelings about our personal situations that work for us. We can use our thoughts to produce riches or poverty, to bless or to condemn, to heal or to make sick, to create things for our betterment or for our detriment. Renowned author and speaker Dr. Wayne Dyer describes our thoughts as "the architects of the foundation of our material world." Our thoughts design and create the groundwork out of which everything in our life emerges.

Look at the things in your life as simply a mirror reflecting back to you what is going on in your inner world, as simply a result of your inner world of thoughts. And understand that what you honestly believe deep in your heart will eventually be known in the external world—you will manifest those beliefs. Thus, if you want to change your outer world, you must change your inner world, as it is inner transformation that brings about outer transformation. Then we are, as Paul the Apostle described, "transformed by the renewing of our mind."

As we work through this process, we begin to realize that nothing we say, think, or do is without its consequence. We become aware of how our thinking acts on us like a boomerang and that we either enjoy or suffer the consequences of our beliefs and actions. With this awareness, we challenge ourselves to think, not merely to react to stimuli. In addition, we establish some guidelines for our thinking—to be positive, constructive, optimistic, idealistic, and enthusiastic. By doing so, we bring new good into our life. Our mind will entertain any ideas we present to it and will give back to us the fruits of that thinking.

Refusing to think negatively dramatically changes our life. The truth is that in every moment we can experience heaven or hell depending on which thoughts we choose to think. Remember the times you chose to replace a negative thought with a positive one? Perhaps you chose to understand rather than to hold a grudge. Or perhaps you chose to believe that something good would come from a difficult situation. By choosing these positive thoughts, did a sense of harmony immediately soothe your entire being? Did you notice that you had more energy and felt lighter? Our negative thoughts and feelings are like weights upon our body and soul.

It takes courage and discipline to practice choosing thoughts that feel good when there is so much around us that feels bad, but ruminating over the negatives is like being stuck in a tar pit. To be free and happy, it is imperative to train our mind to respond to the frustrations of life in ways that serve us, and to make a conscious decision to interrupt our negative thinking. In addition to interrupting our negative thinking, we must refuse to let negative words come out of our mouth. Changing the way we talk is a powerful step in changing our experiences. Highly successful people are very careful about the words and images they use to describe their world. They know that to be a winner, you must think and talk like a winner.

Dr. Norman Vincent Peale was a highly successful person who encouraged us not only to think and talk like a winner, but to see ourselves as a winner. Dr. Peale said, "Formulate and stamp indelibly on your mind a mental picture of yourself as succeeding. Hold this picture tenaciously and never permit it to fade. Your mind will seek to develop this picture." Dr. Peale modeled this so beautifully in his own life as he evolved from being a shy young boy who, he confessed, had "the worst inferiority complex of all" to becoming one of the most influential clergymen in the United States during the twentieth century.

Our positive mental picture reinforces our intention to have the things we desire and makes our belief that we can have them grow stronger. Our beliefs are simply information that we have accepted as true, and, of course, they will always reveal themselves. When we begin to change our beliefs, we begin to change our reality. As we replace old and undesirable ideas with new and more constructive ones, we become victors rather than victims in our life experience.

One of the most common ways we create the experience of victimhood for ourselves is through worry. Worry, which is using our imagination to create something we don't want, comes out of fear. It comes out of focusing on what we might lose or what we want that we might not get. It is imaging things going wrong, imaging a negative outcome, and this imaging of future catastrophes floods us with anxiety. In order to stem the flow of negativity, we can practice catching those worrisome thoughts early and refusing to get lost in them before they become full blown.

Observing our worrisome thoughts and refusing to become lost in them helps them move through us as clouds move through the sky. We can take the position of being a witness rather than an actor in this mind drama we are envisioning. We can observe the drama in our mind rather than identifying with it. As we give ourself some distance from these imaginary mind projections, the easier it will be to remove ourself from this trap. We can also have a gentle, compassionate conversation with ourselves to remind us not to mistake our fear-generated beliefs for facts.

Too many of us get lost in our fear-generated beliefs and live in a state of chronic worry. Chronic worry leaves us constantly stressed and out of control. The world today mirrors stressed people whose thoughts are out of control and rule their behavior. Road rage, according to the American Automobile Association, has increased by more than fifty percent in the last five years. What are people thinking when they are in their car that produces this trance like negative state? Certainly not positive and uplifting thoughts!

Philosopher James Allen wrote, "Only the wise man, only he whose thoughts are controlled and purified, makes the winds and the storms of the soul obey him." We can control and purify our thoughts by putting our attention on those things that bring us joy and by refusing to worry. Our joy lies in our power to choose the thoughts upon which we will dwell thereby creating the kind of lives we desire. Our freedom is in our own thinking.

It is good to remember that our thoughts are like seeds: bits of packaged energy that carry our future. Every thought/seed nurtured in our mind produces its own harvest; the immutable law of life demands that each of us must reap as we sow. Just as we put tiny, dry seeds into soil and they develop into beautiful plants, we can put great ideas into the soil of our minds and develop into beautiful, successful beings.

9

# Dreams and Goals

Author J. K. Rowling said it was her life's ambition to see a book she had written on a shelf in a bookstore. She worked on her first Harry Potter book for five years while a single mother living on public assistance in a tiny Edinburgh flat. While her infant daughter napped, Rowling wrote at a table in a café and kept her vision before her. Her future was not a blank screen. She knew what she wanted, and her clear vision gave her direction and kept her focused.

There were many activities in which Rowling could have engaged while her daughter napped, but she sat in a café and wrote. She did not flit about seeking one pleasure and then another, filling her calendar with excursions and diversions. She remained focused and committed even after several publishers turned down her manuscript. Finally, one took interest. The rest is literary history.

Like Rowling, we can have the pleasure of one day waking up and seeing our dream come true. Turning our dreams into reality begins with being clear and honest about what we really want, because in order to get it, we've got to know what it is. We have to be in touch with our deepest desires before we can make the choices necessary to honor them. Becoming clear about what we want and then making a fierce commitment to achieving that outcome is the most powerful thing we can do to manifest our dream.

What do you dream of accomplishing? What contributions have the circumstances of your life uniquely qualified you to make? Whether you believe it or not, the fact is you were born with incredible potential to achieve extraordinary outcomes, to achieve even that which may appear beyond the bounds of possibility. You have the ability to discover, as Walt Disney did, that "It's kind of fun to do the impossible."

Are you allowing yourself to dream the seemingly impossible? Do you have a dream that ignites your passion? With passionate dreams, you will find your life fulfilling and full. You will find that you have a reason to wake up in the mornings, to greet the day full of anticipation and energy with plans and ideas about what you will do. A heart pulsating with great dreams and passionate desire is the best alarm clock imaginable.

Liz Murray is a person whose heart was pulsating with great dreams and passionate desire. As the child of cocaine-addicted parents in the Bronx living in a home without food, with the presence of drugs everywhere, and with the welfare checks spent before they arrived, Murray's life was bitterly grim. She was fifteen years old when her mom died and she found herself homeless—living on the streets, riding the subway all night, and eating from dumpsters. Determined to take charge of her life, Murray finished high school in just two years while camping out in New York City parks and subway stations. Miraculously, she went on to earn a scholarship from *The New York Times* and entered Harvard in 2000.

Murray's story of going from homelessness to Harvard sounds more like a Hollywood movie than the true story of an intensely determined young woman who dreamed big and refused to give up. Though not a Hollywood film yet, Murray's story was made into a movie by Lifetime Television entitled *From Homeless to Harvard.* I watched an interview with Murray in which she talked of her life on the streets. "I started to grasp the value of the lessons learned while living on the streets," she said. "I knew, after overcoming those daily obstacles that next to nothing could hold me down." Murray's dreams were stronger than the obstacles in the way, and her fierce commitment to her vision inspired her to push through the limitations and to propel her to great heights.

Murray's vision aroused her passion, stimulated her creativity and released her power. Focusing on her vision generated within her an increasing alertness to the opportunities present in her environment and heightened her desire. Her intense yearning became like rocket fuel releasing amazing amounts of energy and creativity. Liz Murray did not just wish for a better life; she had an intense desire for a better life. Just wishing for a better life would have been without effect because just wishing lacks power. It is desire that is the motivating force of life, the generating power of all human action.

Intense desire powered Les Brown from a childhood of impossible circumstances to become an acclaimed motivational speaker. Born on the floor of an abandoned building, given up for adoption, and labeled "educable mentally retarded," he consciously turned tragedy into triumph. Brown considered his goals more than just possible; he considered them necessary. With this "no option" attitude and a total commitment to the hard work necessary, he became unstoppable. With no formal education beyond high school, but with persistence and determination, Brown has distinguished himself as a best-selling author, radio and television personality, and successful entrepreneur. He lives his high-energy message, which tells people how to shake off mediocrity and live up to their greatness.

A powerful way to shake off mediocrity and live up to your greatness is to intensify your desire for your dream through visualization. Visualizing your dream is simply directing your imagination to see your vision in detail until it feels familiar, until you experience it as a reality. It is about getting a clear mental picture of your dream as already accomplished and playing that picture repeatedly in your mind. Then vicariously you experience the difference having your dreams come true will make to your family, your lifestyle, your business, your health, and your enjoyment of life. You will gain clarity as to what the fulfillment of your desires means to you and the purposes and motivations behind them.

Playing that picture again and again in your mind also moves you from a position of positive thinking to positive knowing. Positive knowing takes you beyond just wishing, hoping, or trying to believe something positive. Positive knowing takes you to a place of being intensely convicted that your vision for your future is a reality, not just a fantasy. This positive knowing will put your imagination and the cosmic computer to work for you, and you will find doors opening in a remarkable way. Albert Einstein said, "Imagination is more important than knowledge. For knowledge is limited, whereas imagination embraces the entire world, stimulating progress, giving birth to evolution."

Your imagination has the potential to birth you into the life of your dreams. You can achieve the things you want in life if you have the courage to use your imagination to dream them, the intelligence to make a realistic plan, and the will to see that plan through to the end. Yes, you must make a plan. You can't just leave success to chance. If you don't make a plan, you will just live a rich fantasy life. Without a plan, it is hard to stay the course. You have to have a strategy, a map that will inspire you long after the emotional fuel of willpower is gone.

Designing a strategic plan requires establishing goals. Why? Because goals empower you to control the focus of your mind; they help you develop the skill of focused concentration. Focused concentration gives you the ability to stay on track, to complete the task, to zero in and keep your eye on the target. Developing this tenacity to focus on the target, to not give up, to refuse to let any thing stop you will lead you to success. Focused concentration will also give you the power to overcome all obstacles.

Booker T. Washington said, "You measure the size of the accomplishment by the obstacles you have to overcome to reach your goals." He was a man who knew. As a child, Washington worked in coalmines nine months a year and attended school for three months. Vowing that one day he would study at Hampton Normal and Agricultural Institute, a trade school for blacks, Washington, at age sixteen, walked two hundred miles to Hampton. He worked his way through school as a janitor. Later, he became the first president of Tuskegee Institute and then went on to advise Presidents Theodore Roosevelt and William Howard Taft on racial matters. He also wrote several books, including an autobiography, *Up from Slavery.*

Booker T. Washington committed his mind to his goals. His sense of commitment gave him tremendous inner strength and a clear picture of his own positive future in advance. He understood that great things don't happen until we make a commitment. When we commit to our goals, we become amazingly creative and energized. We find that our goals actually reorder our emotional life and empower us to exercise the self-control and self-direction needed. They become regulators of our behavior.

The function of goal setting as an effective way of regulating human behavior and performance has been extensively researched. This research has shown that goals do indeed increase performance when accompanied by a commitment. However, when commitment drops, performance drops. It is easier to keep our commitment and performance up if we allow the journey to be as much fun as the achievement.

The journey of life is a process to be enjoyed and celebrated each step of the way, so goals work best when they are both process oriented and outcome oriented. Rushing and pushing through life to reach our goals robs us of the joy of the process. Mythologist and author Joseph Campbell said, "We're so engaged in doing things to achieve purposes of outer value that we forget that the inner value, the rapture that is associated with being alive, is what it's all about."

We can reach for our goals from a sense of satisfaction and appreciation for our life, recognizing the amazing gift that it is, and the amazing gifts and accomplishments that are already ours. We don't have to wait until our goals are manifested to feel good. Goal achieving is not about putting off living a full and rich life until we reach them. It's about having a wonderful time along the way, about truly enjoying the process. Moving toward our goals is about savoring the sweetness of the moment and at the same time having an awareness of what the coming days and weeks hold possible for us. It is about planning for the future while capturing the freshness of now.

The process of moving toward our goals is also about allowing the very existence of them to increase our feelings of aliveness, for just as important as the actual achieving of our goals is the vitality and enthusiasm that pulsates through our being in the sheer wanting of them. We can allow ourselves to celebrate the desires within us and to let their very existence fill us with joy and passion. We can pursue them with a sense of playfulness and joy rather than a grim determination driven by feelings of fear or insecurity.

If we find our goals feel like ruthless demands that leave us running after things, always grasping, we need to pause and examine our motivation. When we are driven by feelings of fear or insecurity, our motivation comes from an urge to repair our deficiencies rather than from a desire to grow and to express our creativity. With this motivation, we set ourselves up to feel depleted and stressed. However, if our goals are about expressing who we are rather than proving or repairing who we are, they will energize and rejuvenate us.

Thinking about your goals should fill you with enthusiasm. If not, perhaps they are merely tasks that you feel need to be done. Your goals need to have the component of joy and positive stimulation in them. Writing out all of the benefits and advantages of achieving your goals will allow them to become charged with positive emotion. As you write your goals, allow yourself to enjoy delicious moments of anticipation. The more defined and detailed the goals, the better the aim and focus. Without the specifics, goals are just wishful thinking. Even though you may be endowed with tremendous brilliance, talent, and energy, unless you focus on specific objectives you diminish your chances of accomplishing as much as you are capable. In fact, the reason most people never reach their goals is that they don't define them, learn about them, or even seriously consider them as believable or achievable.

After you've set definite, specific goals, then design a step-by-step plan for achieving those goals. Start with your ultimate outcome and work backwards, letting your immediate actions be the stepping-stones to your ultimate vision. Once you have turned the goals to which you are aiming into a carefully planned journey of action steps, you then have a blueprint. Your blueprint is your detailed plan or program of action. Your immediate actions consist of all the steps you need to accomplish along the way before realizing your ultimate goal. For example, let's say you have established a goal to be your ideal weight and to be in excellent physical shape. Break that goal down into all the steps you need to take to reach it, and then take those steps and break them down into what you need to do on a daily basis. Thus, your daily things-to-do list leads you to your long-range goal. As you take these steps, your confidence will grow and you will build new momentum.

Remember the Chinese proverb: "A journey of a thousand miles must begin with a single step." With small steps day by day, you will soon discover the magnificent life you once believed elusive is the very one you're living. Those tiny choices you make day in and day out are the ones that shape your destiny. Big achievements come one step at a time. You don't have to make massive sacrifices or abandon your responsibilities to go after what you love. What you have to do is discipline yourself to take daily steps in the direction of your dreams. It is just as Henry David Thoreau said, "If one advances confidently in the direction of his dreams, and endeavors to live the life which he has imagined, he will meet with a success unexpected in common hours."

In this process of taking action to move toward your dreams, do not judge each day by the harvest you reap, but by the seeds you plant. Trust that if you take the necessary steps on a daily basis, you will garner your rewards. Give each daily task your absolute best and do not minimize the importance of all those so-called "little things" you do along the way. Helen Keller stated, "I long to accomplish a great and noble task, but it is my chief duty to accomplish small tasks as if they were great and noble."

People who possess such a noble attitude as Helen Keller take continual, bold action. They know that action translates their dreams into reality. Our world is filled with these courageous people. Author Elie Wiesel, viewed by many as one of the key voices of moral leadership in the twentieth century, is such a person. In his autobiography, he shares the remembrance of a dream wherein the voice of an old beggar once came to him, telling him, "Stop dreaming . . . It is time to act." And act he did. Wiesel, a survivor of the Holocaust, and his prolific writings have poignantly reminded us that the Nazi atrocities must never be forgotten, lest history repeat them. When he was awarded the Nobel Peace Prize in 1986, the Nobel

Committee called him a "messenger to mankind" whose message is "one of peace, atonement, and human dignity." Elie Wiesel turned his dreams into action.

As you begin to turn your dreams into action, review your goals everyday and adjust them as you gain new insight and information. Setting goals is not about developing a rigid mindset whereby you don't allow yourself to change directions as you move along. Give yourself permission to be open, fluid, and flexible. Your goals can work against you if you become too attached to having them happen in a certain way or time. Sometimes you have to let go and create new dreams. And often, as you achieve one goal, possibilities will open up that you didn't see before.

Make the necessary adjustments and then persist, persist, persist, or you risk having your dreams go down the drain. Perseverance is essential. One of my favorite stories of persistence is that of Dr. Mary Walker, the only woman to earn the Congressional Medal of Honor and the second woman to graduate from a medical school in the United States. She was unstoppable in reaching her goals.

Dr. Walker wanted to serve as a surgeon in the Civil War but was denied a commission as a medical officer, so she served as an unpaid volunteer. She was a prisoner of war for four months in a Southern prison. In 1865, she was awarded the Medal of Honor but had it taken away in 1917 when Congress revised the Medal standards to include only "actual combat with an enemy." However, she refused to return the Medal, wearing it everyday until her death in 1919. In 1977, an army board reinstated her medal posthumously, citing her "distinguished gallantry, self-sacrifice, patriotism, dedication and unflinching loyalty to her country, despite the apparent discrimination of her sex." Dr. Mary Walker was focused on the great things she desired to accomplish. In doing so, she expanded her vision of herself and transcended the accepted limitations of the day.

Our goals can help us transcend the accepted limitations or status quo as well as the limited perceptions we have of ourself. They can empower us to demonstrate abilities that perhaps we never knew we had and to go beyond our ordinary limits. In doing so, we discover the infinite creative possibilities within us. We begin to understand not only who we are, but also who we can become. Sometimes we may get to the edge of what we think we can do and then shrink back out of fear, thinking we have gone too far. That is the very time to take a deep breath and move on through, and as we do, we will feel our confidence grow. Then we will have the experience of which T. S. Eliot wrote, "Only those who dare to go too far can possibly find out how far one can go."

Creating a larger vision of ourselves and acting upon that vision will enable us to transcend our mental conditioning and circumstances. However, this ongoing effort depends upon an unwavering commitment. The good news is that when we commit ourselves to something greater, to developing the finest within us and breaking through our limiting patterns, something wonderful begins to stir within. We reorder our emotional lives and begin to nourish our potential. Then we begin to experience the advice of German philosopher Goethe: "Whatever you can do, or dream you can, begin it. Boldness has genius, power and magic in it."

From time to time, we may be gifted with an unexpected peak experience that shifts our perception and breaks through our limited thinking, and a sense of boldness fills our being. Peak experiences often awaken us to our innermost longings and create a deep sense of expectancy. They create moments in which the possibilities seem endless. Psychologist Abraham Maslow described peak experiences as moments of great awe and intense happiness, moments of rapture or bliss in which we feel our very best. Most of us have had at least one peak experience in our life. I can vividly recall one of the most joyous and ecstatic peak experiences of my life, which left me with a sense that one day I would meet with "a success unexpected in common hours."

I was walking down Venice Beach feeling so high I thought my heart would explode. Only months before I had picked up the book *Bikram's Beginning Yoga Class* and after studying it, I decided that I wanted to go to California to take yoga classes with Bikram. This was a bold dream for a single mother living just above poverty level. Nevertheless, after only a few weeks of brainstorming, there I was. As I stood on the beach staring at the incredible beauty of the mountains against the infinite sea, my spirits were soaring. Scenes of my future life flashed before me. I knew I was not only going to survive, but thrive. I became totally convinced of my ability to cocreate with God the life of my dreams. This peak experience gave me a fleeting glimpse of what is possible and filled me with joy. I felt so happy that I had acted on a dream and afforded myself the experience of standing on this California beach that was now expanding my vision of my entire life.

The truth is that I hesitated to go to California because I thought it might be a selfish thing to do. How often it is that we have difficulty making ourselves be our own priority for fear of being selfish. It took me a long time to realize that we are all entitled to a higher quality of life, and wanting better is not selfish; it is the by-product of high self-esteem. It takes great courage to act on our own behalf and to live our life as if we really matter. Learning to ask for what we want in life is one of the most important skills we can acquire.

I've also learned that when we are not asking for what we want in life or when we are not going after something we want, there is often a conflict connected with it. It serves us to study that conflict and begin to understand it. If there is a massive gap between what we want and what we truly believe we can have, there is inner work to be done in closing the gap between our desires and expectations. For some of us, our dreams were under too much siege in our early years, so we hid them. Or we derailed our dreams for what seemed to be more reasonable choices. Many of us have creative longings but are too frightened to express them. Instead of letting our fears stop us, we should take a cue from Georgia O'Keefe who said, "I've been terrified every day of my life but that's never stopped me from doing everything I wanted to do."

To move toward our creative longings means taking risks and dealing with the fear that comes with that risk taking. The truth is there is nothing we can do or not do in life that is risk-free. Choosing not to take action is as risky as taking action. Everything involves risks. Once you start taking more risks, you will evolve into a more confident, capable, and stronger person. It is incredibly empowering to accomplish something you didn't believe you could do. Remember the high dive as a child? Or riding your bicycle for the first time? Or taking that first trip by yourself? You took a risk and your confidence escalated.

Give yourself permission to dream and to take the risks necessary to make those dreams come true. Believe that your dreams are possible to obtain. Remember the musical *Man of La Mancha*? The most memorable song in that play is Don Quixote's "Dream the Impossible Dream," which encourages us "to dream the impossible dream, to reach the unreachable star." The truth is that your deepest longing is a possible dream, a reachable star, and it is never too late to start.

One of my deepest longings was to write this book, and I had to overcome much doubt to make it happen. Thankfully, my desire overcame my doubt. I found that the difficulties of my life had served to create within me a passionate desire to share my experiences with the hope that it might help support others in their journey. What passionate desire do you have deep within? Will it make you grow? Will it be good for others?

If we don't have a dream, our life will be about our problems. We will be small-minded and preoccupied with activities that are petty and, for the most part, useless. But when we have worthwhile goals, life has meaning for us. We have a sense of purpose and a sense of direction. We are filled with the joy that comes from knowing where we want to go in life and being on the way to getting there.

One of the best things about knowing what we want and allowing ourselves to have it is that we are much more willing to let other people have what they want. By honoring the ambitions, goals, and personal dreams that keep us inspired and motivated, we will not be preoccupied with how others are living their lives. We will be focused on learning, growing, and being of service. In the process, we will become the great people we were designed to be. As Dr. Martin Luther King Jr. said, "Everyone has the power for greatness—not for fame but greatness, because greatness is determined by service."

If we equate being a success to being of service and design our goals around being of service, our lives will instantly feel more meaningful. Most of us have an innate desire to serve others and not just live for ourselves. We are the happiest when we feel like we are growing and contributing, when we have a sense of dedication to something greater than ourselves. We have learned that one of the great joys of living is discovering something new we can give, something new we can involve ourselves in that makes us even greater contributors to the world. We know that if what we give to the world is far ahead of that which we take from it, we will have lived a triumphant life.

There are millions of us whose major motivation is to help heal and transform the world. We are interested in what we can do for a world that has given us so much.

We want passionately to be extraordinary useful human beings and to make life around us better. We have a powerful human urge to do something significant. We can honor that urge by creating a powerful vision, establishing goals to reach that vision, and then step by step working toward making it a reality. Whether or not we reach our goals, we will always have the inner growth that striving for our goals developed. Growth comes when we aim for our ideal, and not necessarily when we achieve it.

# 10

# Self-Discipline

Imagine yourself to be the twentieth of twenty-two children, born into a poor family in a small Southern town two months premature and weighing only four and a half pounds. Imagine yourself being constantly plagued by illness the first four years of your life, suffering from pneumonia, scarlet fever, and polio. Imagine the polio damaging your left leg so severely that doctors believed you would never walk again. Such was the life into which Wilma Rudolph was born. Rudolph not only learned to walk, but she also went on to become the world's fastest woman, dubbed by the media in the 1960 Olympics as "the Black Gazelle." Throughout her life, she continued to excel in her endeavors, which among many other roles included that of serving as a Goodwill Ambassador to French West Africa.

Self-discipline was one of the main attributes that allowed Wilma Rudolph to overcome the physical problems facing her. However, self-discipline was not the only thing at work. Rudolph's own passionate vision bolstered her self-discipline and gave her the strength to endure the discomfort, monotony, and drudgery that often accompanies self-discipline. A passionate vision paired with self-discipline is the combination that leads to great successes like Rudolph's because that vision allows the "work" of self-discipline to be associated with the possibility of great joy.

It was a compelling vision of winning the Super Bowl that propelled John Elway, known as the Comeback Kid, for all of those last-minute thrilling victories. Elway has won more regular-season games than any other starting quarterback in history and has set numerous NFL records. As he neared his fortieth birthday, he commented in an interview about the many negative questions he was asked concerning getting older. People were questioning if he still had what it took to win. To Elway, it was just a matter of discipline. He simply approached his workouts with total commitment and a willingness to work even harder each year to stay in top physical shape, and his self-discipline paid off. After feeling the sting of losing a Super Bowl three times, he finally experienced his ultimate career dream, not once, but for two consecutive years.

Coaches recruit players like Elway who are committed to winning national championships. They want strong-willed players who have committed to making their dreams come true. They know that players who possess that kind of passion have their eye on a target that keeps them mentally focused. Their mental focus unleashes the power to be disciplined. Whether it is in the arena of sports or any other area of life, outstanding achievers are convinced of the importance of their self-discipline in terms of reaching their goals and making their dreams come true.

Reaching your goals demands discipline. Discipline is requiring yourself to do what needs to be done to obtain the success you desire. It is rising above inner psychological resistance, taking charge of your thinking, and doing the things you need to do. Discipline has been described as the ability to carry out a resolution long after the mood has left you. How many times have you decided to lose weight, or quit smoking, or get in shape, or get organized, or do whatever, only to find that three weeks or three months later things looked even worse? Much of the problem lies in our inability to subordinate our moods to our commitments. Disciplined people realize that there are as many different moods as there are projects, and each project elicits a different mood. Even though they may feel opposition from their mind and feelings toward what needs to be done, they do it anyway.

Our goals are achieved when we exercise enough influence over ourselves to strive for them regardless of how we feel. In his book *The Seven Habits of Highly Effective People,* Stephen Covey gives us a masterful description of discipline. He explains:

> Discipline derives from disciple—disciple to a philosophy, disciple to a set of principles, disciple to a set of values, disciple to an overriding purpose, to a superordinate goal or a person who represents that goal. In other words, if you are an effective manager of your self, your discipline comes from within; it is a function of your independent will. You are a disciple, a follower, of your own deep values and their source. And you have the will, the integrity, to subordinate your feelings, your impulses, your moods to those values.

As we subordinate our feelings, impulses, and moods to our values, we become increasingly self-disciplined, and we take the necessary steps to be the person we desire to be and have the life we want. Unfortunately, however, many people want their life to change but find themselves frequently "not in the mood" to do what needs to be done. They want success but aren't willing to pay the price.

That idea of not being willing to pay the price or not being self-disciplined enough to subordinate one's impulses to a higher goal reminds me of a little incident that occurred around my son's seventh birthday when I took him for his annual physical. Dr. Vernon told Justin he was about eight pounds overweight and counseled him on healthy food choices. On the way home, he was very pensive. Then he said, "Don't worry, Mama, I'm going to take the 'dream-away' pill." I asked inquisitively, "The dream-away pill?" He answered, "Yeah, just take it at night and when you wake up in the morning all the fat is gone. And, if that doesn't work, I'll take Slim-Fast®."

Some people never grow beyond the dream-away pill mentality. They remain in the "instant gratification" mentality, which is a major cause of failure. They want success without an investment. They don't want to do those things that disciplined people do: resist relinquishing an immediate pleasure for a more distant one of greater value.

Most of the things that are best for us in terms of leading to genuine and enduring happiness require us to forgo some immediate gratification. Each time we forgo immediate gratification and get positive results, we build our self-confidence as well as develop new habits. For example, when we come home from work and go for a walk rather than sitting in front of the television eating, we begin a new habit. Then we notice that every positive choice we make attracts and creates other positive choices. If we go for a walk, we may feel an increase in our energy, and now we have the enthusiasm to do other positive things.

Even the smallest action can give us the feeling that progress is being made and increase our sense of optimism and resolve. Most of us have had the experience of taking action to change a habit, and we know how good it feels when we make even a tiny step toward progress. Perhaps we've overcome a pattern of overeating, smoking, procrastinating, or a number of other negative behaviors. We overcame these habits with repeated and sustained practice a day at a time and one step at a time, and in this process, our self-discipline was developed.

In fact, discipline is really about habits. The successful person has a disciplined set of successful habits coupled with high expectations. In his book *Awaken the Giant Within*, Anthony Robbins says,

Any time you sincerely want to make a change, the first thing you must do is to raise your standards. When people ask me what really changed my life eight years ago, I tell them that absolutely the most important thing was changing what I demanded of myself. I wrote down all the things I would no longer accept in my life, all the things I would no longer tolerate, and all the things that I aspired to becoming.

Anthony Robbins raised his expectations of himself; he created new standards. Maybe it is time to raise your standards as to what you expect of yourself, and then discipline yourself to create and engage in habits that will support you in achieving those expectations. Maybe it is time to realize that your destiny is based on your daily actions and choices, and what you do today shapes what you will be tomorrow, and the next day, and the day after that.

Unfortunately, we usually don't change until we get to the point that not changing would be too painful. Most of us believe change is difficult and certainly well worth postponing or preventing if at all possible. I recall sitting at the bedside of a fifty-year-old man whose doctor had counseled him for years to lose weight, exercise, and work at a saner pace. His habits never changed, and now he was fighting for his life after a serious heart attack, praying for another chance.

Maybe you want to be more disciplined in your health habits, but you feel doubtful about your ability to give up some negative behaviors. Feelings of doubt, hopelessness, or inadequacy can keep us from daring to make a change and can cause us to come up with an inexhaustible list of excuses. Our excuses are most often expressions of fear. We fear that we will fail once again, that we don't have the willpower to do what we need to do, or that we will disappoint others and ourselves one more time.

To live an effective life, we must confront our excuses, for we either make excuses or make progress. In my coaching with sales professionals, I've heard tons of excuses as to why they would not make "cold calls." Often I would ask, "Are you afraid?" The immediate reply would be, "No, I'm not afraid, it's just that . . . (and they would name the excuse)." If they were willing, we would process the situation further and find their underlying fear (which was usually a fear of rejection). If they followed this process by taking action and making the calls, they would slowly begin to liberate themselves from the fear. Moreover, they would discover that for every fear faced, there are multiple rewards.

The motivational psychologist Denis Waitley says that one of his mottos is "Stop stewing and start doing." If we don't stop stewing and start doing, we will never know our potential, and we will experience regret. It's like the old saying, "Discipline weighs ounces, regret weighs tons."

We need to take action in those areas of our life in which we are lacking in discipline so that one day we do not find ourselves deep in the sea of regret. We need to do it for ourselves, and we need to do it for our children. Our children desperately need role models of self-discipline, and our example is their starting place. They need to see adults who have learned how to deal with their negative emotions and who exemplify patterns of behavior that reflect their ability to control their impulses.

Children need to see self-disciplined adults doing what they are asking them to do—beginning with simple things, such as being on time, eating a healthy diet, exercising their bodies, keeping their commitments, finishing their assignments, and a host of other positive behaviors. Unfortunately, children see adults behaving as though their internal brake system is nonexistent. They constantly observe a lack of self-control played out on the world stage. Thus, it isn't surprising that one of the biggest trends in schools today is an increase in students' out-of-control behaviors such as anger, aggression, and impulsivity. The cost of such behavior is high and erodes self-respect.

The lack of self-discipline contributes to a poor self-image and loss of respect, while discipline generates self-respect and raises our self-esteem. In fact, the greatest value of discipline is the heightened self-esteem it brings, which makes all the difference in the world in the unfolding of our potential. As we choose to do the things that need to be done, therefore growing in self-esteem, we guide and form our destiny. We lead self-reliant, self-sufficient lives, and we experience the enormous satisfaction and rewards that come from deep within.

In a letter to her daughter who was a student of music, Nobel and Pulitzer Prize winner Pearl S. Buck described this satisfaction. In the book *Pearl Buck*, Ann LaFarge shares the letter. Buck wrote,

> The self-discipline necessary for making beautiful music is the discipline an author needs to write great books, an artist to paint great pictures, a surgeon to perform an operation, a scientist to make a discovery. For that matter, the same discipline is essential for any great accomplishment in life. And the greatest satisfaction comes not from without, but from within. The greatest rewards come not from the discipline applied by others, but from the most beautiful and severe of all disciplines, that which you exert on yourself. . . . The uncommitted life is not worth living; we either believe in something, or we don't.

Pearl S. Buck modeled a person who disciplined herself to take action to those causes to which she was committed. In addition to writing more than one hundred books, she was an indefatigable contributor to humanitarian causes, especially on behalf of orphaned children of mixed American and Asian descent. She also helped remove the stigma from mental retardation and contributed money toward researching its causes. Buck was deeply concerned with issues of racism, poverty, and women's rights and dedicated much of her life to these causes. She experienced the rewards that came from exerting her own internal discipline.

As well as exerting their own internal discipline, achievers like Pearl S. Buck discipline themselves to persevere. They keep on going despite all obstacles. People who give up, however, tend to cast off all discipline and conclude that what they do doesn't matter anyway. Zig Ziglar succinctly expresses the importance of discipline coupled with perseverance when he says, "The major difference between the big shot and the little shot is—the big shot is just a little shot who kept on shooting."

Self-discipline is perseverance in action. Perseverance requires the ability to go on resolutely in spite of difficulties and to train your mind to be unstoppable in reaching your goals. Jim Whittaker, the first American to summit Mount Everest in 1963 and author of *A Life on the Edge,* says, "You can never conquer the mountain, you can only conquer yourself." By conquering yourself, you can do the impossible, for the difference between the impossible and the possible lies in determination and discipline.

Determination and discipline are about making a commitment and then translating that commitment into action gradually. With each action step, you become increasingly determined and disciplined until you reach your goal— you become unstoppable. You will also notice that each success paves the way for more success, and you will find your life moving upward and onward. Henry Wadsworth Longfellow wrote, "Those heights by great men reached and kept were not obtained by sudden flight, but they, while their companions slept, were trailing upward in the night." Commit to "trailing upward in the night" and you will find yourself soaring.

As you soar, you will experience more freedom. The fact is that the more disciplined we are, the more freedom we have. Discipline actually increases our freedom. It certainly increases our freedom from the mental stress of inaction. It also increases our freedom through the increased successes and options that discipline brings. Perhaps most importantly, discipline increases our freedom to involve ourselves in those things we truly enjoy. Once we do those things we do not want to do, we can truly enjoy those things we really want to do. It is like the child who dutifully does his homework so he can go outside and play. It doesn't take much brainpower to figure out that if we use our time more efficiently, we'll complete our tasks more quickly and then we are free to do more of those things we enjoy.

With such a rewarding payoff, self-discipline can be seen as the valuable inner power that it is rather than the restrictive behavior it is commonly thought to be. To attain this inner power, we need to develop the following attributes: determination, perseverance, taking action whether we want to or not, and managing our emotions. These characteristics inevitably lead to self-confidence and self-esteem and consequently to happiness, satisfaction, and success.

# 11

# Attitude

I take pride in sharing the birth date of September 7 with Grandma Moses, for I have long admired her indomitable spirit and zest for living. This remarkable woman lived with astounding vitality, enthusiasm, and productivity until her death at age 101. It was in her one hundredth year that she completed her illustrations for "A Visit from St. Nicholas," which was hailed as some of the finest work of her career. Amazingly, she was in her seventies before she even began her career as an artist, and then she went on to live a rewarding and highly creative life. What an attitude!

Grandma Moses demonstrates that an attitude of positive determination is a galvanizing force, creating the quality of our life. With a positive attitude, we multiply all of our capabilities and opportunities, and we attract good things to us. Nothing is more empowering to our success than a positive attitude. Psychologist William James declared, "The greatest revelation of my generation is the discovery that by changing the inner attitudes of your mind, you can change the outer aspects of your life."

Changing the inner attitudes of our mind often involves summoning our determination to break the bondage of our conditioned thinking and to face our negativity. In doing so, we develop a new liberating set of beliefs about what is really possible in our life, thus altering our perceptions of ourselves and the world. We discover that we have the ability to grow into something greater even if we have been buried in the worst for years.

Mr. T of *Rocky III* expressed this idea of growing into something greater when he proclaimed, "I may have been raised in the ghetto, but there ain't no ghetto in me." Like Mr. T, we can exercise our birthright of free will to overcome the negative barriers regardless of the position in life we find ourselves. We can claim our ability to change our attitude about a situation, for we give our experiences meaning. The problem is that sometimes we want to change our experience of life without changing our attitude. When our mind is inflexible, we find ourselves actually arguing for our limited way of seeing things and seldom see the opportunities around us.

On his eightieth birthday, the celebrated pianist Arthur Rubinstein could have argued for the limitations of his advanced years. Yet he said, "I'm passionately involved in life. I love its change, its color, its movements. To be able to speak, to see, to hear, to walk, to have music and painting . . . it is all a miracle." With this beautiful attitude, Rubinstein lived sixteen more prolific years, enjoying one of the longest active performing careers in musical history.

Our attitudes either propel us forward or hold us back. Arthur Rubinstein chose an attitude that propelled him forward. His attitude mirrored the gratitude and positive expectancy with which he chose to approach life. The fact is that our attitude is simply a mirror of our mind reflecting our thinking, a product of our mental imagery. The way we visualize and think about things in our mind determines how we will feel about those things. Therefore, if we are thinking negative thoughts and seeing negative outcomes, we will have a negative attitude. If we are thinking positive thoughts and seeing positive outcomes, we will have a positive attitude.

The way we think about things will also show through in how we act, for we act according to the mental images that dominate our mind. When we have a "can-do" attitude, we have "can-do" actions. And when we have a "can't-do" attitude, we have "can't-do" actions. Our attitude simply projects on the outside how we are feeling on the inside.

My friend Robert Stribling is possessed by a "can-do" attitude. Fifteen years ago, Robert decided he wanted to meet Sam Walton. However, in the process of dreaming about meeting this prominent man, he noticed some internal dialogue that proposed such questions as "What would keep me from trying to call him? Why would he want to talk with me?" He quickly dealt with these hesitations and devised a plan.

Knowing the finest peaches in the world come from the state of Georgia, Robert sent Mr. Walton a basket of the delicious delicacies with the note, "I just wanted you to know that we appreciate you opening a store here in Macon, Georgia. We're going to do everything we can to support it." In just a little over a week, Robert received a phone call from Mr. Walton thanking him for the gift and adding, "If you are ever in the area, come by and see me." Robert decided he would definitely be in the area.

His next step was to go to the library and do a little research on Sam Walton, preparing himself to engage in conversation that would be of interest to Mr. Walton. He then flew to Arkansas, and once there, stayed in a small motel across the street from Wal-Mart. The next morning, after spending only approximately ten minutes in a waiting area filled with more than two hundred people, Robert received a tour of the facility and a meeting with Sam Walton.

The human resource representative who escorted Robert to meet Mr. Walton was curious as to how he had this privilege when over six hundred people a day call to meet this man. Of course, Robert had this privilege because he established the intention of meeting Mr. Walton, possessed the attitude that he could make it happen, and then took action. Mr. Walton admired him for being such an initiator and told him so as they parted. Shaking Robert's hand, he said, "I appreciate your gumption in coming out here."

An attitude filled with gumption is what it takes to make our dreams come true. Boldness and decisiveness coupled with positive expectation make things happen. Robert's attitude reminds me of the classic children's book *The Little Engine That Could*. Although that little engine was small and had never climbed a mountain before, it wanted to get that stranded trainload of toys to the children on the other side. Fueled by this deep desire and positive attitude, the little engine continually repeated as he struggled up the mountain "I think I can, I think I can, I think I can" until finally he made it over the top.

This "I think I can" attitude develops confidence. As you grow in confidence, you begin to trust yourself to keep doing what you need to do, to keep trying no matter what. You believe in your ability to learn what you need to know to produce the success you desire. Walt Disney was a great believer in the value of confidence and expressed it this way: "Somehow I can't believe that there are any heights that can't be scaled by a man who knows the secrets of making dreams come true. This special secret—curiosity, confidence, courage, and constancy, and the greatest of all is confidence. When you believe in a thing, believe in it all the way, implicitly and unquestionably."

Legson Kayira is a man who, as Walt Disney suggested, believed in something and believed in it all the way. Cynthia Kersey describes Kayira's fascinating journey and unbeatable attitude in her book *Unstoppable*. Legson Kayira was a sixteen-year-old African who decided to walk three thousand miles from his tribal village, north across the wilderness of East Africa, to Cairo, where he would board a ship to America to earn a college education. He took with him a five-day supply of food, a small ax for protection, a blanket, a copy of *The Pilgrim's Progress,* and the Bible. Between his village and Cairo were hundreds of tribes that spoke more than fifty different languages.

It took Kayira two years to reach Cairo. On his way

there, he stopped to work for six months in Kampala, the capital of Uganda. He found a library with a directory of American colleges and wrote to Skagit Valley College in Mount Vernon, Washington. The dean there was so impressed with Kayira's determination that he granted him admission, a full scholarship, and a job that would pay him room and board. Yet, he still had to get to the United States.

The students at Skagit Valley College sent $650 to cover his airfare to America. Finally, he arrived to enroll with the two books in hand that had been his companions since the beginning of his journey. However, Kayira's academic journey didn't stop there. He became a professor of political science at Cambridge University in England and a respected author. He summarizes his experience in this way: "I learned I was not, as most Africans believed, the victim of my circumstances but the master of them."

Kayira's story inspires me tremendously to build an attitude of mental toughness and not to allow myself to feel like a victim of circumstances when facing challenges. His total conviction to handle any difficulty in order to meet with the success for which his heart longed generates within me a sense of determination to be positive and to persist. He is an individual that has modeled for all of us that the key to success is not about the circumstances of our life, but our attitude and response to those circumstances.

With the right attitude, we can bring forth new life out of any set of circumstances. Rabbi Harold Kushner writes in his book *When Bad Things Happen to Good People*, "In the final analysis, the question of why bad things happen to good people translates itself into some very different questions, no longer asking why something happened, but asking how we will respond, what we intend to do now that it has happened."

While spending seven years in a succession of

Vietnamese prison camps, U.S. Naval captain Gerald L. Coffee had to choose his response to these questions in the most horrendous situation. In his deeply inspiring book *Beyond Survival*, Captain Coffee recounts the atrocities of physical torture and psychic stress that he and his comrades had to endure. One week after returning home, Captain Coffee spoke to his church, and among his remarks, he said, "Our lives are a continuing journey— and we must learn and grow at every bend as we make our way, sometimes stumbling, but always moving toward the finest within us." The most fulfilled people are those who do indeed move toward the finest within them, who resourcefully, creatively, and realistically master their ability to choose their response. These people are governed by a positive attitude and a determination to stand up to conditions rather than to give in. They are the Captain Coffees of the world who courageously model for us that while it is not possible to control all that happens, we can control the impact events have on us.

The founder of Mothers Against Drunk Driving (MADD), Cindy Lightner, transformed a tragedy into a remarkable contribution to society. When a drunk driver killed her twelve-year-old daughter, she began an outreach that has educated, informed, and changed our world. Her attitude to rise above being a victim, even amidst the most tragic and painful circumstances, is deeply inspiring. Though I'm not sure that Cindy Lightner would describe herself as an optimist, her response to her tragedy is characteristic of one, for optimists look for positive ways to deal with life regardless of what has been handed them.

Rather than condemning the negative circumstances in their life, optimists look for ways to transform them. They tend to focus on the possibilities, on the solutions, and they maintain an attitude of positive expectancy. Yes, optimists see the problems, but they keep their focus on the outcomes they desire. Optimists know that to achieve a breakthrough the focus must be on the solution rather than the problem, for focusing on the problem only makes it grow bigger and more ominous. They are aware that focusing on the problem produces stress and sets them up for a negative attitude.

On the other hand, pessimists tend to focus on what they can't do or what they are afraid will happen. Their mind keeps sliding into those well-worn patterns of catastrophizing, replaying old hurts and flashing pictures of the worse-case scenarios. Pessimists stay stuck in their pain instead of moving forward to a positive future. To a pessimist, only the gloomy side of things is reality. The biggest challenge a pessimist has to deal with is the sense of helplessness and hopelessness that tends to permeate their very being. The pessimist has to come to understand that the feeling of being helpless is just that . . . a feeling. Optimists know this. They know that they can temporarily feel helpless without defining their entire being as helpless. They know their feelings are not permanent. An optimist knows that though the sky isn't always blue, it isn't always gray either.

Pessimists, alternatively, can be presented with the best information in the world, but with their deep-seated belief that the odds are stacked against them, they will feel there is no use in even trying. They will even try to make the information wrong. A pessimist can have all the talent and desire necessary for success, but their pessimistic approach to life sets them up for failure. Pessimism is crippling and stifles aspirations.

The good news is that pessimism is escapable. You can choose not to trap yourself in the trance of negativity. Becoming an optimist is a matter of choosing your focus, changing the way you look at things, and developing an attitude of positive expectancy. It is a matter of making it a habit to look for the good. You can choose to think about those things that make you feel good. Even making the choice to feel good, to really want to feel good, is a mindset that can steer your attitude in a positive direction. The challenge is to focus on the things that empower you, as your focus greatly shapes your attitude. When you focus on positive aspects, the negative things lose their power.

Unfortunately, many people expend their energy focusing on the negative and, as a result, experience very little happiness. Be wise enough not to focus on what brings you unhappiness. When you turn away from your tendency to be negative and move toward the positive, you free yourself to become highly productive in the world. Moreover, your confidence grows with each and every battle you win over those negative thoughts swirling in your head.

Anne Frank might be described as one of the greatest optimists in history. She was thirteen years old when her family went into hiding, and for the next two years, she never left the building she called the Secret Annex. Frank lived in the midst of history's most brutal and inhuman event, the Holocaust, and she described the horrors of that war in her diary. Though the last years of her life were lived in the most wretched conditions imaginable, in one of her last diary entries, she wrote, "In spite of everything, I still believe that people are really good at heart."

Helen Keller was another extraordinary optimist—a woman who was an absolute master at focusing on the possibilities. Although she became blind and deaf at the age of nineteen months due to a damaging brain fever, she went on to graduate with honors from Radcliffe College and to become an author, lecturer, and humanitarian. Her dedicated work had an international influence on the lives of the handicapped and changed the course of history for millions. Helen Keller succinctly expressed the idea of focusing on the positive when she wrote, "So much has been given to me; I have no time to ponder over that which has been denied."

When, like Helen Keller, we begin putting our attention

on what's right in our life, we open to infinite possibilities and create positive outcomes. But when we focus on the negatives and the things that we are powerless to change, and make them the source of all of our problems, we are limiting our entire future. George Bernard Shaw wrote, "People are always blaming their circumstances for where they are. I don't believe in circumstances. The people who get on in this world are the people who get up and look for the circumstances they want, and if they can't find them, make them."

However, some people go through life continually changing circumstances in their pursuit of happiness only to find themselves unhappy and searching once again. The problem is that their unhappiness is generated more by their attitude toward themselves and life than by their circumstances. Though some circumstances do indeed need to be changed, for the most part our inner world needs some adjustment. To experience joy, we do not have to depend on anything outside of us. In fact, as Anne Frank demonstrated, joy can be present in the most difficult circumstances and the most unlikely places. As Marcel Proust wrote, "The real voyage of discovery consists not in seeking new landscapes, but in having new eyes."

Emme is a woman who had "new eyes" when it came to breaking through the cultural stereotypes of beauty in our society. Wearing a size sixteen and weighing 190 pounds with a height of five foot eleven, Emme believed that true beauty "absolutely comes in every size, shape, age, and color." With her confident attitude, she has become an enormously successful plus-size model, influencing scores of women with her feel-good, look-good philosophy, particularly the nearly half of all American women whose body type Emme reflects.

Emme could have limited her aspirations to be a model by accepting society's prejudice against plus-size women. It would have been easy for her to feel like a victim of such prejudice, for it is easy to believe that what we experience is due to external causes over which we have little or no control. But the reality is that for those of us living in a free country with an abundance of opportunities and resources, the circumstances in which we find ourselves correspond with our habitual attitude. We can change our circumstances and discover freedom when we creatively take control over our thoughts, fears, and reactions and refuse to feel helpless.

Learning to say no to feelings of helplessness and to approach life with the unrelenting attitude that somehow things will work out if you hang in and conquer the challenges facing you is enormously empowering. This attitude can be cultivated. One of the ways to cultivate it is to concentrate on what you can do rather than focusing on what you can't do or how bad things are.

Instead of feeling helpless upon hearing the news that millions of landmines claim thousands of victims every year, Jody Williams focused on what she could do. Williams became the founder and chief organizer of the International Campaign to Ban Landmines. She has dedicated much of her life to assisting the innocent wounded by war and the prevention of further such atrocities. Williams is one of only ten women who have received the Nobel Peace Prize and only the third woman from the United States. Upon receiving this great honor, she said, "The most important thing to understand is that in order to create the world you want to live in, you must take action to bring about the changes you want to see in the world."

The world is full of good people like Jody Williams, great humanitarians that really care, people who donate every dollar they possibly can, and people who stand up, take action, and speak out to make a difference. Nevertheless, we are bombarded with the negativity in our culture since the media is determined to show us every pocket of despair. We read the newspaper and our heart breaks repeatedly. The horrors of human experience are laid before us each day. We have to remind ourselves that for every act of violence or greed there are thousands of acts of love and generosity. The dark side of human nature is far outweighed by the energies of goodness and compassion.

Certainly, the dark side of life and the defeats we will inevitably experience bring us down from time to time. If defeats in life didn't temporarily deflate us, it might be a strong indication that we aren't emotionally involved with life. It is natural to feel despondent now and then. The question is not whether we "get down," but how long we stay that way. Frustration is a natural part of our life experience, but we must not become stuck in it.

One of the most important skills you can develop is learning how to talk to yourself when you feel stuck or experience personal setbacks. You simply must not allow thoughts that weaken you. You must consciously choose empowering thoughts that give you confidence and encouragement. You must choose to believe in yourself and that something inside you is bigger than your circumstances. Marie Curie stated, "Life is not easy for any of us. But what of that? We must have perseverance and, above all, confidence in ourselves. We must believe that we are gifted for something, and that this something, at whatever cost, must be attained."

Julia Child was a woman who believed she was "gifted for something." In Noel Riley Fitch's biography of Julia Child, *Appetite for Life,* Child discussed her size as a 6'2" tall woman wearing a size twelve shoe. She said, "I was always one size bigger than you could ever buy." Even so, she did not let her unusual size interfere with her zest for life and commitment to doing what she loved. "I decided," she said, "why languish as a giantess when it's so much fun to be a myth?" And a myth she became, imparting her famous cooking techniques as a television personality and author until her death at age ninety-one.

Like Julia Child, we can accept life on its own terms, focus on our strengths rather than our weaknesses, and expect good things to happen. Our expectations have a potent influence on what shows up in our life, on whether or not we produce desirable or undesirable consequences. For example, we may want our dreams to come true, but in reality, we expect much less. Our dreams might feel too big or too impossible, or we may even feel undeserving of them. The fact is that we will get what we expect and feel deserving of, though it might not be the dream we desire.

Understanding the relationship between our attitude, expectations, and beliefs can help us discern our role in creating our attitude. Our attitude comes from our expectations. If we have positive expectations, we have a positive attitude, and vice versa. Our expectations come from our beliefs. A belief is simply a habit of thought, a thought we keep thinking that filters our perception of the world. What we believe is what we see; our reality is the product of our beliefs. The world we create will always reflect our deepest beliefs. Since a belief is the mental acceptance of some idea as being true, we have the power to change our beliefs.

The placebo effect profoundly demonstrates the power of our beliefs and expectations. The fact that an inert substance can cure a person of illness, so long as the person believes they are taking an effective medicine, is truly amazing. Not only do these medically useless pills have an effect on a patient simply because the patient expects it to, but they have the exact effect the patient expects of the medication. The patient's expectation is so strong that it actually causes something to happen. This is convincing evidence that a change of attitude can indeed shape every cell and tissue of our body.

Undeniably, our internal chemistry is intimately connected with our patterns of thinking and feeling. Neuroscientists have learned that thoughts are electrical impulses that trigger electrical and chemical switches in the brain, affecting the chemical activity of the brain and immediately releasing appropriate chemicals into the body. Consequently, a thought is very much a physical event, a piece of chemistry that affects our entire body. Every thought we think activates molecules in our brain and is transformed into physiological impulses that instantly change our biology. For example, when we experience fear, our mind produces molecules that show up as adrenaline.

Scientists are increasingly learning how the body and mind mirror each other, how our cells respond to our mental patterns, and how we converse with all the cells in our body. We are learning that this miraculous human psychochemistry is not a system beyond our control. We are learning that intentionally changing how we think and behave can have a profound impact on our brain chemistry.

In addition, our attitudes cause emotional reactions that strongly affect our immune and circulatory systems and our risk of accidents. In fact, our psychological state can change our immune response. Exactly how this works has yet to be precisely determined, but many groundbreaking studies in the science of psychoneuroimmunology continue to confirm this fact, as well as give evidence that our thinking can enhance our healing powers or depress and weaken them.

For instance, despair depresses immune system responses, while feelings of hopefulness bring about psychological and physiological changes that strengthen the body's resistance. Studies have also shown a link between feelings of chronic helplessness and a reduction in immune functions including natural killer cell levels. It has long been known that the emotions created by fear, worry, resentment, and hate can lead to many physical illnesses. Scientific evidence appears to validate what the author of Proverbs wrote centuries ago: "A cheerful heart is a good medicine, but a downcast spirit dries up the bones."

An example of how this downcast spirit can affect us is the phenomenon in medicine tagged as "dying from the diagnosis," which is described as a death caused by hopelessness. Hopelessness leads to fear, which can produce death—physically, emotionally, or spiritually. When some patients learn they have a disease such as cancer, they immediately believe they have been given a diagnosis of hopelessness. Hopelessness puts us in a passive state, making us less likely to take the steps we need to improve our situation. Hopelessness often leads us to believe there is nothing we can do to change what happens to us. This, of course, is not true. Our power of choice gives us the ability to affect and influence outcomes.

When experiencing hopelessness, it is important to choose to keep moving and resist that passive state. If we keep moving, we discover we have the ability and resources to handle the pain and anxiety, and not only do we survive, but we often thrive in the midst of the distress. The possibility of thriving in the midst of distress exists because it is frequently in our so-called defeats that we discover our strengths. It is in our biggest challenges that we have the opportunity to dig deep within and find the inner resources to help us deal with the hurt and disappointment.

When you are positive and determined in the center of challenging circumstances, others notice and admire that quality, and your attitude is a gift that offers inspiration. Casey Stengel, one of the greatest baseball mangers in the history of the game, inspired his fans with his antics and with the way he maintained his spiritedness even in defeat. Stengel used defeat to advance and always looked for victory. Though his greatest fame came from managing the Yankees to ten pennants and seven World

Championships, his colorful, enthusiastic personality won him the hearts of the public. When he died at eighty-five, the *New York Times* wrote, "Charles Dillon Stengel's face was heavily wrinkled, his ears were floppy, his voice was guttural, his endurance beyond belief."

Akin to Stengel, we can use our defeats to continuously advance rather than allowing them to plunge us into negative, grouchy moods that have no rewards, only unpleasant consequences. We can use each day of our life as an opportunity to be cheerful, loving, kind, and positive. Elevating our mood is not only a gift of kindness to others, but it will also help us make better decisions and act more intelligently.

How we treat the world is how the world treats us. By maintaining an attitude of positive expectancy, it is within our reach to live a fulfilling and joyful life, wondering what interesting people and beautiful sights will cross our path.

# 12

# Personal Power and Problems

I still remember that very moment many years ago in which I was blindsided by a crisis that catapulted me into pain and confusion. Suddenly I found myself dealing with a devastating betrayal and an ensuing divorce, which led me into a valley of darkness and despair. Life as I had known it suddenly ended, and I temporarily lost my sense of safety and trust.

A pervasive feeling of brokenheartedness stayed with me for a long time. I felt emotionally stretched far beyond where I thought I could or wanted to go. The good news is that much later when I regained my sense of self, I was someone else. I was someone stronger, someone more determined to love and accept myself, someone less willing to use my relationships as the reflector of my worth. I learned that I could hold more than I held before, I could bear more than I thought possible, and I could be more than I ever dreamed. I came to realize that, as Wayne Dyer writes in *Wisdom of the Ages,* "Every sinking into despair has within it the energy to move us higher."

My experience in this abyss of despair provided me with an opportunity for a deeper level of healing within myself. Suddenly I was called upon by life to confront and overcome a well of unacknowledged fears lying dormant in my consciousness. I realized I depended on the love of my husband to feel safe in life; I gave him my power to feel secure. I came face to face with the truth that until I overcame my deeply rooted fear of abandonment, I could never be the master of my fate. As I moved through this process of healing, I developed a much deeper and broader view of life and myself. I came to view the entire experience as an incredible transformational process that opened me to a new vision of myself. Most importantly, I developed the strength and courage to see myself through my own eyes and not through the eyes of another. I faced the certainty that I alone, in the most fundamental sense, am responsible for my own life.

This great loss brought forth a great gain in terms of my own personal development as it created a space in which new visions and perceptions began to appear. The English writer Charlotte Brontë once wrote, "A depressing and difficult passage has prefaced every new page I have turned in life." Perhaps there is a less painful route to new beginnings, but like Brontë, I certainly see these difficult passages as a theme in my own life.

If we view our losses as opportunities for "a new page" rather than great tragedies, we can use them to expand our consciousness and as junctures to move us to the next level. We can also use our losses to develop courage, for sustaining misfortune gallantly when our heart is aching with pain and suffering requires great courage. When we face those occasions in which life just hurts, when things feel overwhelming or unfair, we can choose to allow ourselves to be open to the gifts of our experience. We can choose how to handle these inevitable challenges.

Tough times are intrinsic to life. Despite our best efforts, pain and vexing problems come up. In *How to Get What You Want and Want What You Have*, John Gray addresses those inevitable problems. Gray writes:

> Personal success is not an imaginary state of grace devoid of conflict, disappointment, or frustration. A big part of mastering personal success is learning how to transform negative feelings into positive feelings and negative experiences into lessons learned. Being true to yourself is

a growing process involving much change, which includes experiencing life's ups and downs. Achieving personal success means that when you fall down, you will know exactly how to get back up.

Most of us, however, would agree with Lucy in the Peanuts cartoon: "I hate ups and downs. I just want ups." Though we know that life has moments of both great joy and great sorrow, we would just prefer the joy, thank you! But no matter what we prefer, "downtimes" will occur, and sometimes the lows last so long that it feels as though this dark night of the soul will never end.

During this time, it is often difficult to believe that this darkness could be a prelude to a greater experience of life, or that we have any ability to choose our response to this pain and suffering. We just feel overwhelmed. However, these overwhelming feelings of pain have the potential to catapult us to an internal journey that will direct us toward a new understanding of life's meaning and purpose. In fact, it is often pain and suffering that brings the motivation for exploring the real meaning of life.

Suffering can serve as the wake-up call that leads us to new self-awareness and the asking of fundamental "life questions" about what we want and what our values are. Suffering can force our attention toward places in our psyche and soul that we would normally neglect and give us glimpses of other ways we might want to be in the world. It can shift how we see ourselves and how we see others and transform us into being a more compassionate, gentle person.

"A deep distress hath humanized my soul," the poet William Wordsworth lamented in his "Elegiac Stanzas." Wordsworth was referring to the drowning of his favorite brother, John, who was the captain of a sailing vessel. Supposedly, Wordsworth suffered such a shock that he did not speak for two months. Afterwards, he produced a new kind of poetry defined by a deeper, more reflective, and less romantic tone. The experience changed how he saw the world, thus changing what he offered to the world through his poetry.

As Wordsworth discovered, crisis has the potential to uproot our old perceptions. Sometimes the despair that crisis brings suggests that the time has arrived for far-reaching changes in how we expect to find happiness and greater fulfillment in life. We are moved out of our rigidity. We find ourselves being led to better circumstances and discover that the crisis was a stepping stone not a crushing stone.

Crises don't look like opportunities when we are in the midst of them. But diamonds don't look like precious gems in their rough, unpolished state. Yet, the pressure is applied, and the diamonds are created. We have the choice to allow the pressure in our own lives to either enhance or tarnish our growth. We can choose to believe that going through the darkness will give us the opportunity to be the light.

Remember as a kid when you would just slightly shift the kaleidoscope, and then all the patterns would change? Life is like that. One moment we can feel a sense of calm and happiness, and then the slightest change alters everything. When that change occurs, it is important to remind ourselves that this is a temporary state and, most importantly, that we can shift the kaleidoscope through our interpretation of this low cycle.

I'm always working with myself to shift my mental response to problems and adversity and to look for the opportunity. My history has been to dive into self-pity and feel victimized. Learning to ask myself during difficult times "What can I get out of this that would enhance my life and the lives of others as well?" empowers me and opens me to new possibilities. I try to remember that the obstacles and fears that I am encountering are not an accident; they are the very challenges I need to promote my unique growth. I remind myself that my problems are messengers telling me what needs to be loved, what needs to be seen more fully.

Problems help us learn what we need to learn. The lessons we refuse to learn are presented to us time and again until we conquer the root cause of our struggle and grow psychologically and spiritually. We can gain inspiration and increase our awareness of how to use our problems to evolve by studying the lives of those people who have surmounted every conceivable obstacle—heredity, environment, lack of education, physical handicaps—to create great success.

It lifts my spirits to read of individuals with remarkable attitudes, such as Helen Keller who said, "I thank God for my handicaps, for through them, I have found myself, my work, and my God." Imagine this coming from a woman who became deaf, blind, and severely speech-impaired as a baby. She possessed this attitude at a time when there were precious few resources available to her. Although Helen Keller had limited vision, she realized she had unlimited potential.

John Milton, who out of the dark isolation of blindness brought forth *Paradise Lost,* also realized his unlimited potential. Moreover, in the starkness of a prison cell, John Bunyan wrote *Pilgrim's Progress.* Beethoven did not let deafness end his career as a composer; he emerged from the crisis with a series of triumphant works that mark the beginning of a new period in his stylistic development. As the outer world receded for him, he turned inward and probed the mysteries of life in a new musical language. At the premier of his "Ninth Symphony," he had to be turned around to *see* the applause he could not hear.

I am strengthened by those who have taken their personal misfortunes, and through their courage, given inspiration to millions. Facing unusual challenges requires finding greater-than-average sources of energy and inner resources that often result in superior performance and contribution. It is said that Harriet Tubman returned to hell to bring others out, and as Kemp Battle comments in *Hearts of Fire,* "Such is the true heroic journey." Like Tubman, we can do more than survive the tragedies of our life; we can use them to help create a better life for others.

What we can learn from people like Harriet Tubman, Helen Keller, and John Bunyan is to let our challenges be springboards. Even in the grips of our deepest pain, we can stay determined to grow and learn from our experiences. We can create something meaningful out of everything life hands us. Disappointments do not have to stop us. In fact, disappointments and obstacles can make us stronger than we ever dreamed possible. The philosopher Friedrich Nietzsche wrote, "Whatever does not destroy me makes me strong." Furthermore, Joseph Campbell said, "Any disaster you can survive is an improvement in your character, your stature, and your life. What a privilege!"

We can learn to be resilient people who are able to face our trials and tribulations of life without being overwhelmed or defeated by them. We can learn to escape our problems, not by running away, but by overcoming them and working our way through them. This is resiliency, and resiliency is essential to success. Look at your past and find the evidence that supports how strong, resilient, and truly creative you are. Take it in and let it inspire you. Look at all the times you were challenged and successfully managed the difficulties. Look at all the times you did not allow your problems to cause suffering, when you understood that the pain you were experiencing was your reaction to circumstances. There is an amazing connection between the way we look at things and what we actually experience. How we think will bring us either relief or aggravation. We can curse the darkness or look for the lesson. We can see opportunity, or we can see trouble.

In times of difficulty, we often experience a death of some aspect of ourselves. We grow through sequences of death and rebirth. These sequences are actually enlightenment processes. As we die to the old, we awaken to new and more powerful aspects of ourselves. The glorious fact is we can always die to the old and have a new beginning. We can let each second be a new birth experience. The real barriers and limitations we meet in life are not out there; they are within. It is time we begin telling ourselves that we are equal to the task. We can learn to roll with the punches rather than struggle wildly when the blows of unavoidable disappointments strike.

Forming the habit of finding value in your disappointments and pain can bring you comfort. Ask yourself if there is some other way you can view the problem or if there are any new messages you can give yourself about the situation. You can also allow your negative feelings about what is going on in your life be the launching pad to something you want. Use your frustration to launch your rocket of determination. Translate your frustration into new energy.

Our history shows us that courageous people use even the most tragic of events to benefit the lives of others. Two of the worst disasters in the history of space flight occurred on January 28, 1986, as seven astronauts on the Challenger Space Shuttle died on their way to space, and on February 1, 2003, when the seven astronauts aboard the Columbia flight died on their way home. Much of the world witnessed these catastrophic events on television. A devastating sense of grief and emptiness blanketed the world at the loss of these brave explorers.

A few months after the Challenger accident, the families of the seven crew members traveled to Arizona where they met with educators from across the nation to decide how best to memorialize their loved ones. They used this great personal tragedy to make things better.

As a result of that meeting, the Challenger Center for Space Science Education, an international, not-for-profit organization was founded. Its mission is to continue the crew's educational undertaking—to learn, to explore, and to inspire. To date, there are more than forty learning centers. The focus of this terrible failure became one of learning from our mistakes and honoring the ones who paid for those mistakes.

In learning from our mistakes and trying again, we demonstrate a boldness that refuses to be intimidated by failure. We use failure as only a turning place in the road, an inevitable part of the process of moving forward. We act courageously, believing that every failure in life offers the opportunity to evolve to another level of awareness, and we look for the substance and meaning in what didn't work. We don't give up if we fail.

Of course, the fear of failure is probably the main reason many of us don't even try. This is operating from the "if you don't try, you won't fail" attitude and an effort to find success by avoiding failure. However, failure and success are intricately intertwined. In order to do something well, we must first be willing to do it badly. Fear of failure is one of the biggest obstacles to success. It is also the biggest trap that keeps us from taking action.

Those of us who are parents watched our babies fall down frequently as they learned to walk. Falling down didn't keep them from getting back up and trying to walk again. They didn't just give up the chance to walk and, ultimately, to run. Just like the baby, we can accept failure as a chance to try again with renewed self-confidence and determination. Ideally, every time we experience a failure we learn from it. The simple process of correcting what isn't working is exactly how we learn.

We can't progress unless we make mistakes. Failure only becomes failure when we do not learn from it. As we examine what didn't work, we refuse to label our lack of success as failure. We know that even if we have failed in some endeavors, failure does not make us a failure. Defeat is never a fact unless accepted as such. If we see ourselves as a failure, we create a self-fulfilling prophecy. With that self-image, we will unconsciously sabotage our efforts. We must perceive ourself as a successful person learning from our mistakes.

Unfortunately, some people have such rigid mental rules that no matter what they do or what they learn from their experiences, they see themselves as a failure. They expect themselves to produce impeccable results without the trials of mistakes. They set themselves up for letdown by harboring impossible expectations that are utterly ruthless in the pressure they put upon them.

Impossibly high goals and expectations prevent our acting upon and attaining goals that are humanly possible and satisfying. We must choose a set of humane premises to live by. We must be in touch with the limits of human possibility to reach a compassionate level of life. And we must spend more time contemplating the solution rather than the problem.

Too often we hug our problems like a security blanket. We won't let them go because they give us an excuse for behaving in ways that are self-sabotaging. As strange as that may sound, we are often resistant to letting go of our excuses and changing our behavior. We find it easier to blame and feel victimized than to assume total responsibility for our lives. Thus, we continue to approach our problems with the same old worn-out excuses and behaviors that didn't work in the past.

We need to be willing to assume total responsibility for our problems and then shift our attention in the *direction* of the solution. We often can't shift our attention to the exact solution because we don't know the solution, but we can shift it in the direction of the solution. This begins to open a channel through which our solutions will come. As we focus on what we want to achieve, doors will open and solutions will come. Our experience changes by focusing on what we desire rather than the problem.

Learning the art of keeping your mind focused upon the things, conditions, and circumstances you really want is essential. Contemplate the perfect outcome to every situation in your life. The picture you form in your mind should be so clear you can almost touch it, and it should be projected with feeling. Use this process of visualization to magnify your desires. Creative visualization is a powerful tool for seeing a positive outcome, which, in addition to creating that outcome, helps you to overcome discouragement and not be defeated by it.

You are already using creative visualization—your imagination—every minute of the day. The important question becomes "Are you using it to create the life you desire, or to magnify your fears?" Whenever you engage in positive-possibility thinking, you are using your imagination to envision desirable outcomes. You are attracting to yourself the opportunities and circumstances to which you aspire, and the solutions appear.

Sometimes it is in the most unusual circumstances that our imagination is stimulated and we feel encouraged to press forward until we successfully meet with our positive outcome. A story in the picture book *Do All Spiders Spin Webs?*, by Melvin and Gilda Berger, tells how a spider inspired a king and helped win a war. According to the Bergers, the tale is as follows:

In the year 1306, Robert the Bruce, King of Scotland, was at war with England. Once, after losing six battles in a row, the king hid out in a barn. While there, he noticed a spider trying to swing on a thread from one beam to another. Six times he saw the spider try, missing the beam every time. But finally, on the seventh try, the spider succeeded. Inspired by the spider, King Robert came out of hiding and returned to his troops. This time he won and was able to drive the English out of Scotland.

As this little story illustrates, we often mount our greatest determination when we retreat from our battles and allow our imagination to take flight as we regroup and renew our commitment. We rise to a higher level of thinking and allow the obstacles to tap into our deepest strengths and abilities. Our creativity begins to expand in unexpected ways, and because of the challenge, we become wiser and more confident.

In *The Road Less Traveled*, M. Scott Peck writes, "Wise people learn not to dread but actually to welcome problems." Welcoming our problems opens us up to finding treasures in them and the opportunity to envision with greater clarity the outcomes we truly desire. Welcoming our problems allows us to see the ways in which we need to grow in our own consciousness and to see potential gains rather than fearful losses. When we do so, we often become surprised at how much we've gained in what we thought were losses. Our challenges actually proved to be rungs on the ladder of our personal evolution that we grabbed onto as we pulled our way higher.

Facing and working through our problems and fears allow us to gain great freedom. This process allows us to become more conscious of those things within us that hold us back and to become aware of the "payoffs" of holding on to our problems and problematic behavior. By "payoffs," I am referring to the reward obtained for engaging in seemingly undesirable behavior. While it may seem insane to derive pleasure from a behavior which brings pain, on some level it is rewarding.

We are surrounded by examples of undesirable behaviors that bring payoffs. Many overweight people continue their negative eating habits because the food brings pleasure though being overweight is painful. The child who acts out in school is consistently punished yet continues the behavior because it brings attention. Some people chronically pout to get their way even though pouting causes them to shut down and experience negative emotions. We all have behaviors in our lives that we cling to, even if they create problems, because they have some payoffs. However, we might not be conscious of those payoffs.

The ideal is to become conscious of these false rewards so we can make healthier choices in meeting our needs. However, we tend not to deal with these problems lest we lose the benefits. One of my chronic patterns was that of self-pity. The unconscious payoff was that it kept me in my comfort zone and allowed me a distorted way of dealing with my pain when I had no skill in understanding how to be compassionate with myself. I actually gained this understanding from reading an article by poet and author Stephen Levine in which he wrote, "Pity arises from meeting pain with fear. Compassion comes when you meet it with love."

We experience true joy in living when we learn to accept with equanimity both the pain and the gifts of life. With the acceptance that life is far greater than our human minds can begin to grasp, we acknowledge that much of what happens in life will always be beyond our comprehension. This awareness helps us to be compassionate both to others and to ourselves. Our personal pain can help us cultivate compassion for the pain that we all share. Max DePree writes in *Leadership Is an Art,* "In a difficult and fractured and complex world, in problems of failure and of success, but especially in the joys and tragedies of our personal lives, we touch each other. This 'touching' is at the heart of who we are."

Adversity can have the effect of expanding us and sharpening our sight, allowing us to touch each other more deeply. During those times in my life when my heart felt particularly broken, it seemed as though I attended to things more closely, like the shadings of the trees, the flowers, the sky, the expressions on people's faces. It all appeared to be more vivid, to present itself with greater luster. It was as though I was shaken out of any complacency. In the words of Ralph Waldo Emerson, "When it is dark enough, men see stars."

When you experience dark times, meet your challenges with courage and the best you have to give. As difficult as it may seem to do, sometimes you simply have to refuse to dissolve into the misery of the situation. When the going gets tough and everything in you feels like giving up, have the courage to persist. Have the courage to rise to the occasion with as much determination, dignity, and energy you can muster. If you keep going, the ideas will come and the skies will clear, and you will achieve your goals.

# 13

# Healing Addictions

Some years ago, Oprah Winfrey fascinated us with her impressive weight loss only to gain it all back. In her courageous and open style, Winfrey admitted that she dealt with the symptoms without dealing with the core issues. She showed us that modifying the behavior doesn't necessarily cure the disease. During one episode of her show, Winfrey shared how she is now learning to feel and manage her emotions and her addictive thinking without medicating with food. Her openness with her struggle is inspiring.

As Winfrey came to understand, stopping the addictive habit doesn't necessarily stop the addictive thinking. In fact, it rarely does. And although it is imperative to cease the acting out, recovery is more than just about refraining from unhealthy behavior. Recovery is about looking at the distorted thinking and feeling that it is connected to that behavior. Healing addiction is about feeling what we have been trying to avoid. Otherwise, we will return once again to indulging in pleasures and distractions of every description to escape our anxiety and inner pain.

We have a multitude of ways of going unconscious to avoid our feelings. The use of food, alcohol, drugs, relationships, sex, work, shopping, and other fleeting euphoria-producing behaviors are paths that millions of us mistakenly choose in seeking to find happiness and to alter our mood. Our addictions are methods we use to move toward pleasure, though some of us aren't even attempting to feel high. We just want to reduce the anxiety, escape the pain, and feel normal.

The goal of the addicted personality is that of achieving pleasure and relieving discomfort. Thus addictions, whether involving compulsive behavior or the use of chemicals, become our mood adjustors. They become obsessive-compulsive behaviors that distract us from feelings we want to avoid. In other words, they become a way to block emotional pain. Addictions essentially serve as a way to escape, a salvation from life's challenges or the emptiness inside. But the solution soon becomes part of the problem as the obsessive-compulsive behaviors only make matters worse because of the shame and guilt they generate.

It is our resistance to emotional discomfort that causes us to anesthetize ourselves so we won't have to feel. Then we walk around numb, unable to feel any pain or experience the joys of life. We have deadened ourselves. To complicate matters, our culture encourages us to numb ourselves with activity, consumption, or entertainment. It fosters addictive thinking with its instant gratification philosophy and technology. It encourages the mind-numbing and isolating effects of television and other electronic opiates.

This instant gratification philosophy enables us to satisfy our desire for immediate gratification at the expense of our personal dignity. In fact, it encourages this impulse-control disorder (another name for addiction), leaving us living at the mercy of our desires and intolerant of delays. As we act out our addictions, compulsively trying to get our fix, our self-esteem dips lower and lower. Nevertheless, our longing for pleasure keeps us hooked.

This deep longing for pleasure, for feelings of comfort and security, lies at the heart of addiction. We turn to our addictions when we believe we cannot find these feelings any other way. As we satisfy our desires through a particular person, substance, or activity, we experience gratification. When this becomes a habit, we become dependent on or addicted to that experience. We seek the intoxication of that experience. Moreover, we continue the behavior in spite of bad consequences because our compulsions drive us to do in excess anything that feels good or brings a heightened sense of gratification.

Along with that deep longing for pleasure, there is a gnawing emptiness within. We search, believing there is something we need to get in order to feel fulfilled, in order to feel in control, in order to relax. We keep looking for pleasure in the wrong places, trying desperately to grasp from outside the love, satisfaction, and pleasure that we crave. Yet looking for meaning and happiness outside ourself only leaves us feeling more insecure and anxious. So, in spite of all our methods of seeking satisfaction, we continue to feel unsettled and unfulfilled.

Some of us feel compelled to mix the good with the bad in order to feel pleasure. We feel compelled to create drama because this is what we have known; this is what we grew up with. Addictions satisfy this need by keeping us on the roller coaster between pleasure and pain, with peaks of elation followed by valleys of despair. We then find ourselves engaging in compulsive rituals to ward off the despair once we lose the high.

Eventually we discover that although these compulsions and addictions provide temporary fulfillment, they lead to suffering as well. Ultimately, they block our serenity and fulfillment and cause more pain. We discover that it just doesn't work to try to buffer ourselves from the pain of life through the valium of temporary pleasures. Even so, our addictions seem to hold a spell over us. They feel like some powerful secret at the center of everything we do, and they steal our freedom by consuming our time and energy, leaving us feeling powerless.

For many years, the powerful secret at the center of my being was relationship addiction. Not only did my relationship dependency hold a powerful spell over me, but it also created fertile ground for full-scale drama. I unconsciously needed chaos in order to feel normal, and my unhealthy relationships supplied me with plenty of chaos. They also supplied me with the illusion that my unmet needs for safety and love, which have ruled most of my life, would be fulfilled.

Since my very survival felt based on finding someone or something to fulfill those basic needs, I felt like a puppet whose strings were controlled by external forces. I was constantly engaging in manic attempts to fill the emptiness. Any moment not spent being incredibly busy or distracted or obsessing about a relationship would trigger just how lonely, sad, hurt, and mad I really was. Therefore, I kept the drama going and became addicted to my own adrenaline.

My pattern was to "save" someone in order to feel good about myself, which I hoped would lead to getting the love I needed. Unfortunately, I repetitively attached myself to emotionally unavailable men whose primary form of communication was withholding. I would then become obsessed with trying to open the door to their hearts. In addition, I consistently chose partners who caused me pain and embarrassment, and then either I made excuses for their lack of consideration, bad tempers, or put downs or I convinced myself I could change them. I never knew love unattached from pain and suffering, so I played the victim role for a very long time.

My low self-esteem left me conflicted as to whether I had legitimate expectations of my relationships, or whether I was just possessed by selfishness and an inability to handle disappointment and frustrations. If I was able to convince myself that my expectations were too high, I allowed myself to accept all forms of unacceptable behavior and to continue my addictive patterns. In looking back, I can see that some unconscious part of me felt that I deserved to be treated in a critical manner. I was also not conscious of my willingness to settle for just being needed since

I did not feel loveable. In fact, being needed fed my addiction, because I didn't feel I had any value apart from being valuable to someone else. And once that someone was gone, I ceased to exist, because I had no identity of my own.

This lack of self-love and self-worth enabled the codependency to thrive. In fact, low self-worth is the very foundation of codependency, for it leads to addictive thinking. Addictive thinking is the way we counter feelings of unworthiness, the way we try to find something to empower us. This faulty thinking tells us the power we need to be successful is not within us but somewhere else. We become obsessed with that someone or something else that has our power, and we establish a compulsive relationship with it. This compulsive relationship has us repeating self-destructive behaviors and going back to what is familiar even though it might not be healthy. The desire for an anesthetic to dull the agony dominates our behavior. It is an agony that comes from a lack of self-love, and we have endless ways of hurting ourselves when we don't accept and value who we are. One of the ways we hurt ourselves is by remaining in unfulfilling and painful relationships. We keep ourselves in a victim role, and then feel angry, hurt, and helpless.

Fortunately for me, I became aware of my addictive behavior when, in the late eighties, Robin Norwood's book *Women Who Love Too Much* hit the bookstands and rapidly became a bestseller. I painfully found myself on almost every page, and for the first time, I was introduced to the concept of relationship addiction. What an awakening to realize that to avoid my own painful feelings of unworthiness I was literally "fixing" with relationships, using them as my drug of escape. Never had it occurred to me that I was an addict. Up until that point, even after years of therapy, I knew nothing of the disease of addiction.

Recently I reread *Women Who Love Too Much*, and I

realize, of course, that it's not just about women, and it's not about love. We can't love too much. But at that time, I finally had a context for my obsession with relationships and for my attraction to wounded and distant men. Once I could see my unhealthy behavior as manifestations of the addictive process, I had a clearer understanding of what I needed to do to recover. Today I question what my recovery would be had I continued to be in therapy without some education about addiction.

My passionate new interest in the subject of relationship addiction, which I began terming as "codependency," led me to workshops and seminars. I read everything about the topic I could get my hands on. I talked to therapists. I attended groups. I attended Codependency Anonymous and Adult Children of Alcoholics meetings and eventually found many of the answers I had been seeking. Finally, I assumed my most important and my most neglected responsibility: taking care of myself.

For most of my life, I had assumed the duty of worrying about other people and trying to save them from their pain at the expense of my own needs. I called this behavior kindness, concern, and love. Now I call it codependency. I learned to use the word "codependency" as a description, not a negative self-judgment. I learned to have compassion for my faulty ways of loving instead of harshly criticizing myself. But this compassion toward myself was very difficult to summon and took much time.

I made the commitment to make my recovery from my addictive behaviors my first priority, and, slowly, I began to learn how to promote my own well-being. Behaviors that once felt normal and familiar began to feel uncomfortable and unhealthy. Gradually, I began to stop doing those things that kept me sick. Initially, it was very frightening to be myself without trying to please or act in ways that seemingly gained the approval and love of others. But after years of staying with the process, I found that relating as

I genuinely am brought sweet relief, and my life started working.

Slowly, I stopped placing the power of my personal estimation of myself in someone else's hands. I stopped giving my power away. I stopped trying in vain to get from others what I was not giving to myself, what I felt was missing in me. It became clear to me that as long as I needed someone or something outside myself to make me "feel whole," I was not giving myself the love I needed from me. So, with one tiny step at a time, I began to learn to love myself. I also began to understand some other reasons behind my addictive behavior by asking myself hard questions. Why did I stay in relationships that I knew were painful and abusive? Why did I hang on long after it was healthy to do so? I came to understand. Actually, I came to feel. I came to feel the paralyzing effect of my deep fear of abandonment. I came to feel the intensity with which my fear of rejection drove me to compulsive behavior. I got in touch with how I bonded with others through my neediness, and how my sense of incompleteness drove me to connect in unhealthy ways.

After beginning to feel these things, I became more aware of why separating from relationships was enormously difficult for me. The fear of loneliness and the fear of being unloved was so great in me that I became a slave to that fear. Regardless of how troublesome a relationship, I would cling. Rather than end it, I became more intense in fixing it. I was willing to give up my true self and toss my values aside to meet someone's desires, hoping to gain companionship and a feeling of love.

When we feel an intense dependency on something or someone, we are inevitably afraid of losing that thing or person. Then we begin to obsess. Obsessing means we are full of fear. Our fear drives us to extreme measures, to control so we won't experience the hurt and pain inside. We may try to control by instilling guilt and fear in others to make them do what we want. We may try to control by having emotional meltdowns that result in our getting our way, or we may use more subtle methods such as manipulation. Controlling may give us some temporary relief from our fear, but it never works in the end.

Feelings of emptiness fuel controlling and clinging behavior. Feelings of emptiness are a disconnection from our true self. When we split from our authentic self, chronic feelings of emptiness, sadness, and confusion pervade our life, and we search in vain for someone or something to fill the void. Feeling deprived, we become driven to the high of a relationship, the power of money, or the applause of an audience. We may seek the comfort of food or the ecstasy of sex—anything to bring fulfillment. Sometimes we shift our addictions such as substituting religious rapture for romantic passion, using spirituality to cover up our feelings. It's easy to distort our natural propensity for transcendent experiences into addictive behaviors. Sadly, we're substituting sensation for true joy.

Eventually, we begin to spin out of control with whatever relationship, substance, or activity we have chosen as the answer to our problems, though we are often in deep denial about our increasing sense of helplessness. In fact, the addict's major tool of delusion is denial. Denial allays anxiety. It enables us to maintain a sense of self-control. It sets the trap that there is no problem, and it keeps us from seeing, thus keeping the addiction cycle going. Denial occurs when our psychological system shuts us off from the realization of truth because we feel so overwhelmingly threatened by it.

Denial provides a temporary reprieve. Brenda Schaeffer writes in *Love Addiction,* "The addictive person does whatever he or she can to avoid difficult situations or to suppress problems or to blame them on others in order to return to a false comfort as quickly and easily as possible. Addictions provide momentary relief, but conscious, fearless living provides true solutions to problems and long-term relief."

Living in denial prohibits change, and that brings us comfort, for on some level we know that releasing our addictions will change our life. And we are resistant to change. In fact, much of denial is due to intense resistance to change. We struggle between going backward or bursting on through to a new way of being. We justify our addictions, and then we come to believe in our justifications. We have a long list of excuses for ineffective living. We tell ourselves that being with someone is better than being alone, or that we can't afford to make a change, or that the timing is not right. Our excuses simply delay our improvement, and they keep us trapped.

Healing can't occur until we break through denial, face the anxiety, and learn to deal with it. If we don't learn how to manage our anxiety, we will continue to use various addictions to try to change how we feel. We will continue medicating, which only keeps us wounded and immature. As a matter of fact, our emotional maturation stopped at the point that our addictive behavior began. Hence, we may find ourselves with a forty-year-old body behaving like a sixteen year old. We have to deal with the feelings surrounding our "developmental arrests" before we can grow and flourish and become emotionally mature. Not dealing with our emotions contributes to our inability to maintain an addictive-free lifestyle.

Breaking through denial, the first step toward healing, allows us to admit that there is something in our lives that needs healing. Being unwilling to admit that fact to ourselves means we are just kidding ourselves. Acknowledging the truth releases the energy that was used to contain or deny. Sadly, it may take hitting rock bottom before we come out of denial and develop the passionate desire to reconstruct our lives. Some of us have to almost drown in self-destruction before our egos are shattered enough to face the truth and have us admit we are out of control.

Facing the truth and transforming our lives involves learning how to let go of the things we thought we couldn't do without. It is about making a conscious decision to move away from those people and behaviors that are toxic to our long-term good, and toward those people and behaviors that support our growth. Healing from addiction is about changing. It is not about wanting to change; it is about *doing* it.

Moving away from negative behaviors and relationships is not the only change an addict must face. The addict's major challenge is altering and healing a distorted self-image. Without healing the distorted self-concept, recovery is difficult to maintain. The road to wholeness is knowing your value and unconditional self-acceptance. You relapse when you forget your worthiness. You relapse when you put yourself down. You relapse when you live with the same old outworn patterns of behavior that keep you from evolving. Ridding yourself of the old habits you do not want comes with repeated and consistent action. Only by not following those habits of negative self-talk, fantasy, and escape are you left facing the actual problems of your life. Do not think you are being deprived of something when you stop your addictive behavior; you are in fact giving yourself freedom and dignity. People who work a program of recovery are often times more honest, self-aware, and responsible than the majority who haven't chosen to be accountable.

Recovery also involves developing new patterns of fulfillment in addition to ridding yourself of old habits. The process of change and recovery requires getting in touch with your own internal sources of joy, nurturing yourself, and attending to your emotional and spiritual growth. It requires learning to focus on yourself and learning to give yourself what you have been trying so desperately to get from things outside of you. Recovery is also about accepting that there is only one person you can change and that person is you. We often try to control the lives of others to avoid facing our own issues, but we can lose our mind trying to change anyone but ourselves. I heard speaker and author Byron Katie address this idea in a seminar: "I am so busy thinking what you are thinking that I have lost my mind." Katie was talking about how we can get so obsessed trying to figure out what is going on with another that we lose our emotional health. We must redirect the obsession of changing others into our own life and our own recovery. When we do, we learn that trying to change other people doesn't bring happiness but changing ourselves does.

Changing yourself requires an ongoing commitment to self-awareness, making conscious choices, and staying keenly aware of the consequences of your choices. As you make wise, conscious choices on your behalf moment by moment, you become stronger and feel more empowered to face your challenges. In addition, as you become increasingly aware, the less you live impulsively, and the less you will retreat into escapism. Gradually, through recognizing your power of choice, your addiction will loosen its power over you.

If you can get yourself to quiet down enough to see the mechanics of addiction and your opportunity for choice, addiction loses its grip. With nonjudgmental awareness, you can simply experience what is happening internally without acting compulsively on your desires or suppressing them. You can look with compassion and gentleness for where you can intervene in the sequence of the compulsion. You can learn to replace automatic, programmed responses with aware, healthy actions and find positive ways to fulfill your needs. Let's say you have a habit of compulsively eating. Rather than grabbing food when the desire arises, you can make a choice to sit, breathe, and feel what is going on inside you. Perhaps you feel anxious and scared. At this point, you can decide either to act on your compulsion to eat or to find a healthier way of dealing with the anxiety and fear.

You can also empower yourself to intervene in the sequence of the compulsion by taking your unfinished business from its hiding place. As you make the unconscious conscious, those feelings lose their powerful grip on you. You learn that if you allow the painful feelings, at some point they will dissolve. However, you may find initially that it is difficult to identify your feelings and to communicate them. This was certainly true for me. I actually had to learn how to get in touch with my true feelings. I was surprised to discover how disassociated I was from my inner world. That's what we do when we fear our feelings. We shut down and numb out.

All of these aspects of recovery require allowing ourselves to be vulnerable enough to let others support us. I have received tremendous support for my recovery for which I will be eternally grateful. Some of the very best help were programs at Onsite, a healing center in Tennessee. Onsite was established by Sharon Wegscheider-Cruse and later purchased by Ted Klontz and Margie Zugich. These beautiful people have helped thousands to heal, and their center continues to be an outstanding organization for recovery. The first program I attended, "Learning to Love Yourself," was powerful in helping me to recognize my strengths, my value, and the ability of my choices to create an even greater life for myself. In that safe environment, I began to identify and communicate my painful feelings of low self-worth. Releasing the years of repressed hurt provided me with the ability to experience new levels of joy, pleasure, and vitality.

It was also at Onsite that I was introduced to the idea of being "spiritually disabled" as the inability to connect with oneself in any meaningful way, which is a result of chronic low self-worth. I came to understand how being out of touch with our inner life sets the stage for addiction and how recovery is essentially about unearthing our true self. Our true self can emerge only if we give it our attention. Until we find ways to reconnect with the essence of who we really are and to experience pleasure in our life apart from our addictions, we will find it enormously difficult to give them up. Recovery begins when we realize that no external activities or substances can satisfy the void within, and we accept the challenge to rediscover our true self and find our joy inside.

The workshops of Jacquelyn Small have also been of great help in my recovery. Small offers a soul-based healing program through her Eupsychia Institute, which focuses on psycho-spiritual processes such as integrative breathwork, guided imagery, symbolic artwork, and journaling. Her teachings emphasize overcoming ego issues so we can live more from our souls and honor the healing force within us that constantly urges us toward realizing our greatest potential. It was in one of her workshops that I came to truly understand codependence as a process many of us go through as we learn how to love. I began to see codependence as a spiritual issue, a place in our evolution we must move beyond.

These programs, and many others, support the fact that complete and lasting recovery requires abstinence and spiritual growth. If we do not abstain, we cannot grow spiritually. And if we do not grow spiritually, we cannot remain abstinent. Psychiatrist Carl Jung called alcoholism "the equivalent of the spiritual thirst of our being for *wholeness.*" He believed the only hope for recovery was a profound change of the spirit, that a spiritual awakening is necessary for addicts to get well.

When you lack spiritual sustenance, you are truly hungry and thirsty. As you grow spiritually and learn to fill your inner hunger and thirst with your own love, your addictive burdens will fall away. Trust that as you stay on the path of recovery, you will succeed. It doesn't matter how many times you have failed to stop your addictive behaviors, refuse to give up. Center your attention on what you want and know that you are stronger than your addictions.

# 14

# Love and Forgiveness

Fred Rogers was a person who knew the impact of love. As a young man fresh out of college, he felt disturbed by the poor nature of children's programs, so he looked for work in the field of television in order to do something about it. He wanted to develop a show devoted to the subjects of love, acceptance, and tolerance and the concept of human worth. And indeed he did. *Mister Rogers' Neighborhood* was the longest-running children's program on public television, and Fred Rogers proved to be one of the most respected and influential figures in American broadcasting. For more than thirty years, he told his young viewers that "helping love grow is the most important thing we can do."

Mr. Rogers's simple words were a statement of great wisdom, for what could be of more value than to help love grow. The greatest achievement of any life is to love well; in fact, our ability to love is the truest barometer of our success. Jack Kornfield writes in *A Grateful Heart,* edited by M. J. Ryan, "At the end of life, our questions are very simple: Did I live fully? Did I love well?"

We all long to live fully and love well, for love is our very essence. Love is something we absolutely must express to feel that life is really worth living. Something in us knows that when we've missed dedicating our heart and soul to loving, we've missed the essence of life, we've missed experiencing life's greatest treasure.

When we withhold our love from others or ourselves, we feel miserable, since our happiness equates to our capacity to love. Indeed, our happiness equates more to our capacity to love than to being loved because happiness is the result of love flowing through us. In fact, as adults, we benefit more from the loving thoughts we send to others than from the loving thoughts that others send us. Other people can love us, but that does not necessarily make us happy. What makes us happy is expressing the love that is the very essence of our being.

However, when we are not in touch with the love that is the very essence of our being, we begin shopping for love, approaching love as if it's "out there." We go around as if we are empty people waiting to be filled with love rather than people filled with love that is wanting to be expressed. We hunt for the love we think we need, forgetting that love is something we already are, and not something we must get.

If we are not shopping for love, many of us are trying to earn it. We think of love as a commodity—something we can gain through our behavior. Some of us grew up believing that love was a reward we would receive if we were good. We believed that if we could just be perfect enough, we would be loved. We did not experience love as something inside of us; we were waiting to "get it."

Our experience with love and happiness can only begin to change when we realize we are "it." Thinking of ourselves as people who have love to give rather than as people who must "get it" is a dramatic shift and moves us from looking *for* love to looking for opportunities *to* love. As we look for opportunities to love and develop our capacity to love more fully, we not only experience greater happiness, but we extend that happiness to those around us.

My most joyous opportunity to love has come from being a mother. This has been my most important life role, so when I stumbled across a paper my son wrote when he was fourteen years old that affirmed the love he felt from me, I was thrilled. Justin wrote a short essay for an English class assignment about "Home." My heart melted and tears of joy flowed when I read his opening: "My home is small, but it is filled with big love. My mom and I are the only ones who live there. We love each other."

I was so happy that my son felt our little home was filled with "big love." It helped me to feel that as a mother I had been successful in helping him feel valued, safe, respected and empowered...because that is how we feel when we are in the presence of love. Being in the presence of love is a joyous experience...an inspiring one.

To be in the presence of love can also be a healing experience. The healing power of love is more than a notion; it is an actual physical reality. During a research project at Harvard Medical School, a professor showed students a film of Mother Teresa lovingly caring for her patients. Analysis of the students' saliva for antibodies (a measure of immune response) before and after the film showed a measurable increase in their immune response following the film. In addition, research has shown that love activates certain aspects of the "relaxation response" as well as blocking aspects of the stress response. Dr. Dean Ornish, author of *Love and Survival*, said that if a new drug had the same impact as love, virtually every doctor in the country would be recommending it for his or her patients—that it would be malpractice not to prescribe it.

Love is the highest, fastest, and most healing energy in the universe—the greatest power, a force like no other. Lauren Manning states the power of love saved her life. On September 11, 2001, Manning stepped into the lobby of the World Trade Center moments after the first plane hit and, in a split second, was engulfed in flames. Doctors said she had a 10 percent chance of survival, after being burned over 82 percent of her body. Manning vowed to live for her husband and baby son.

In his book *Love, Greg & Lauren,* Greg Manning, Lauren's husband, recorded the first harrowing weeks after 9/11 when his wife hovered precariously between life and death. With his wife in a drug-induced coma, Greg sat by her bedside telling stories, playing music, and reading poetry, particularly his favorite poem: "My Love is Like a Red, Red Rose." As Greg stayed by her side through the long, difficult days praying that she would awaken, he discovered anew the depth of his love and admiration for the woman who became his hero. Greg Manning practiced the art of loving in the toughest of times.

Unlike Greg, some people can only maintain feelings of love when things are "ideal." They have no tolerance for people or situations that test their patience, frustrate, or inconvenience them. Their love tends to be narcissistic, a love that is only offered when it is convenient and feeds their ego (a "what's in it for me" approach). They tend to base their love on the emotions or impulses of the moment.

Certainly, our strong positive emotions of regard and affection are involved in loving, but they cannot be our only criteria, for love is not mere sentiment. Genuine love is coupled with action—deliberate, purposeful action with the intention of promoting the well-being and happiness of another. The very nature of love is the desire to bring joy and happiness through giving, caring, and sharing without a hidden agenda. We may endlessly declare our love, but unless our actions support it, our intentions are questionable.

Our actions support our love when we consider others' needs and act for the highest good of the situation. Or when we help others grow and become stronger, or respond to their weaknesses by wanting to support or help them in any possible way. Our behavior is loving when we seek to make others feel important rather than looking to them to make us feel important. Our behavior is loving when we seek to experience the mutual enjoyment and pleasure of give and take and allow others to be the end focus of our love, not the means.

Unfortunately, many of us have unconsciously used others to get what we want and labeled these relationships "love." One of the biggest traps we fall into is using others to make us feel whole, to fill the deprived places within us. These relationships often begin with infatuation—a state of excitement and euphoria that gives us a high and produces great expectations. Infatuation is a bubble that will inevitably burst because it is possessed by idealized images that have little to do with reality. With such unrealistic expectations, we soon find that the ideas we have about how we want someone to love and fulfill us lead to disappointment and pain. Disappointment and pain happen because no one can possibly give us all the love we desire in just the way we desire it regardless of how hard they try, or how desperately they may want to. Nor can we do that for others; it is an impossible task.

When the bubble bursts, we begin to feel disillusioned, and we think love is gone, but, in fact, it is the illusion that is gone. With the illusion gone, real love now has an opportunity to grow. This growth can happen if we choose to look realistically and honestly at ourselves and do the necessary "inner work" that love requires. Inner work involves looking at the unmet needs and deep patterns that we bring to relationships with a willingness to transform these patterns.

Learning to love does indeed involve deep work. It requires great effort to transform ourselves into people who express love in both emotions and actions. This effort can be compared to the work of an athlete who spends years in persistent trainings in order to bring his body and skill to perfection. Just as with the athlete, proficiency in our ability to love grows and develops by practice until it comes through in our actions more and more frequently.

Developing the ability to love is an art that must be practiced, particularly when things are not sweet and easy. The tough practice of love involves learning to love others even when they can give nothing in return, or when they are not a member of our inner circle. It involves continually releasing our fears and opening our heart to those who have hurt us, to those whom we feel anger and blame.

Being a loving person requires looking for what is good and loving. Often we must look beyond our habitual judgments to see the goodness that is there. We can't be loving while we are judging, criticizing, or blaming. These negative thoughts—these defenses—are created out of fear and only serve to inhibit our ability to accept or reciprocate the love we so deeply desire. For example, if we have a deep fear of rejection, we unconsciously push others away with our criticism. We are trying to protect ourselves from getting hurt. Or maybe we judge our children harshly to protect ourselves from feeling our own inadequacies as a parent.

Having compassion for the frightened part of ourselves generating this fear and a willingness to heal our fears empowers us to be the loving people we desire to be. If we do not choose to heal our fears, we will move through life too frightened to fully express and experience the love within us. We will also move through life not loving, accepting, or knowing ourselves, which will impede our ability to love others.

We will also find it difficult to engage in caring behaviors. Although the very nature of our heart is to care, our fear gets in the way of caring. But we can learn to break through our fears and honor our heart's desire to care, and do whatever we can to make someone else's life a little better. We can show our caring through such behaviors as listening, comforting, and being patient, honest, and responsible.

While a senior in college at the University of Georgia, I met a remarkable woman who dedicated her life to the spiritual practice of love. Peace Pilgrim had trekked across most of the United States and Canada for nearly thirty years living and speaking the message to "overcome evil with good, falsehood with truth, and hatred with love." She had given up all her worldly possessions and decided to live only in the present. She had absolute trust that God would provide. Written in an old college notebook that I had on the day I met Peace Pilgrim are the words "live to give instead of living to get."

Those who are filled with love "live to give." The good news is that we are living in a time when so many individuals are committing themselves to the spiritual path of loving and giving. Many of us recognize that the world will not survive unless we learn to love one another, so we are working toward shifting the collective conscious from fear and separation to unity and love. We know that love overcomes feelings of separation, and it is only when our hearts are closed that we have the illusion we are separate from each other.

When we love, we connect with the deepest part of ourselves and the deepest part of others—the essence of our being. To live from this essence in love for others and ourselves is life's greatest challenge and greatest opportunity. In fact, all of our life lessons are essentially about learning to master the ability to love.

To love others can be particularly difficult when we feel we have been hurt and betrayed. Lorraine Hansberry's play *A Raisin in the Sun* tells a powerful story of love maintained during a time of betrayal and great sorrow. The play depicts the dreams and frustrations of a black family seeking to escape the ghetto life of Harlem. When the older brother loses part of the family's $10,000 inheritance, their ticket out, he returns home to break the news that their hopes for a better life have been stolen. In hearing this, his sister lashes out at him, calling him every despicable thing she can imagine. Their mother interrupts and says, "I thought I taught you to love him."

The daughter answers, "Love him? There's nothing left to love." The mother responds:

> There's always something left to love. And if you ain't learned that, you ain't learned nothing. Have you cried for that boy today? I don't mean for yourself and the family because we lost all that money. I mean for him: for what he's been through and what it done to him. Child, when do you think is the time to love somebody the most: when they done good and made things easy for everybody? Well then, you ain't through learning, because that ain't the time at all. It's when he's at his lowest and can't believe in himself 'cause the world done whipped him so. When you starts measuring somebody, measure him right, child, measure him right. Make sure you done taken into account what hills and valleys he done come through before he got to wherever he is.

Lorraine Hansberry is not only speaking of love, she is also speaking of forgiveness. If we really want to love, we must learn how to forgive. When we withhold forgiveness, we withhold love. When we don't forgive, the doorway to our heart is closed. Martin Luther King Jr. noted the connection between love and forgiveness when he said, "We must develop and maintain the capacity to forgive. He who is devoid of the power to forgive is devoid of the power to love."

Blaming, bearing grudges, and judging others in any way inhibits the flow of love. Forgiveness is the choice to release our judgments and our interpretations of the motives of others and to do our best to understand those that hurt us. The poet Henry Wadsworth Longfellow wrote, "If we could read the secret history of our enemies, we should find in each man's life sorrow and suffering enough to disarm all hostility." Sincerely trying to understand helps us find some compassion for actions that are infuriating and intolerable, and this understanding can open the door to forgiveness and love.

Opening the door to forgiveness is the beginning of a process with a rhythm and dynamic of its own that is unique to each of us and is not to be forced. Forgiveness will come after we have fully felt the truth of our feelings and released our own hurt. Forgiveness is a process of acknowledging the hurt (not minimizing our own pain), expressing our anger and sadness, feeling it fully, grieving, and letting go. Anger is constructive when it is acknowledged, dealt with, and used to bring about a positive change. We can take the energy of anger and set it in a healthy direction.

Forgiveness is not about suppressing our hurt and anger and pretending the injustice never happened. By suppressing our anger, we suppress the energy it provides to propel us forward. Trying constantly not to be angry binds us to it. The suppressed anger becomes rage, which is layers and layers of unprocessed anger. Suppressed anger can also become resentment, which is buried anger that is relived in our mind. Resentment is really a form of attachment that keeps us chained to the rock of suffering and weakens us. Holding resentment toward another binds us to that person by an emotional link that is stronger than steel and creates the desire to punish or get even. Resentment is doubly destructive, as this old Yiddish phrase makes clear: "When you go out for revenge, you have to dig two graves."

When we harbor personal resentment, hatred, or prejudice of any kind, we handicap our own life. In the words of Ghandi, "An eye for an eye makes everybody blind." We have to refuse to operate with an "eye for an eye and a tooth for a tooth" mentality.

Louis Zamperini's autobiography *Devil at My Heels* is a compelling story of a man who refused to operate out of a retribution mentality. Zamperini was a bombardier in World War II whose plane was shot down over the

Pacific Ocean. He survived forty-three days on a raft, only to be rescued by the Japanese and sent to a particularly brutal prisoner of war camp. There he was humiliated and tortured until the end of the war. After the POW experiences, Zamperini was plagued by nightmares and swore to take revenge on his Japanese tormentors. Then, at the request of his wife, he went to hear a young preacher named Billy Graham and his life was changed. In 1998, he returned to Japan for the Nagano Winter Olympics and carried the Olympic torch through the very village in which he was held prisoner. He systematically sought out his captors, not to seek vengeance, but to forgive. In 1999, the Worldwide Forgiveness Alliance named him a "Hero of Forgiveness."

Zamperini knew that to be free, he must forgive. To be happy, we must forgive. To move forward in our life, we must forgive, else we are stuck in the past. Forgiveness is allowing ourselves to "get past the past," so we can enjoy our present moment and stop poisoning it by continually replaying and dwelling on the injustices we have suffered. Forgiveness is relinquishing our grievances and grudges, so we can feel good inside our own skin. It is an act of self-love, an act of being compassionate enough toward ourselves to release the pain and suffering. Forgiveness is actually our own release mechanism from suffering: we don't hold grudges; they hold us. They hold us captive to our own negative energy. We sacrifice our happiness and the quality of our life by not forgiving and end up punishing ourselves.

The inability to forgive is usually coupled with blame. Blame is a toxic emotion that sabotages our success, makes us feel like a victim, and generates self-pity. Blame typically has a pay-off; it keeps us from being responsible for what is showing up in our life. It is often easier to blame another person for why our life isn't working than to accept personal responsibility.

I recall having a session with a man who wanted to spend our time together blaming a former employer for all the resulting turmoil in his life after losing his job. He announced that he could never forgive this employer. My efforts to discuss his job-seeking attempts and his future possibilities were futile. He seemed intent on replaying and rehashing old hurts, though he was approaching almost a year of unemployment and potential bankruptcy. After much discussion and a slight penetration of his defenses, I learned that he had never put a résumé together and had only been on two job interviews. I could sense his fear of job seeking and the rejection that might involve, but he refused to have that conversation. He also refused to discuss any guilt for not taking initiative in seeking employment and the impact that had on his family. However, he did want to continue talking about his hatred toward his former employer.

If we choose to deal with the fears and guilt that revolve around taking responsibility for our life, we can relinquish the blame that holds us prisoner. Then we might be faced with the supreme forgiveness—forgiving ourselves. Forgiving ourselves for the ways we have failed to show up in our own life or for the negative choices we have made are essential for our freedom. It is also essential in our ability to forgive others. If we can forgive ourselves of our so-called failures, then we can forgive others for their failures. Our own self-attack and self-judgments drive us to judge and attack others and to want to be right always. It is neither intelligent nor kind to want to be right all the time, and it prevents us from connecting heart to heart.

Connecting heart to heart enables us to see each other beyond our egoistic defenses of fear and pride. It enables us to see how vulnerable we truly are and awakens the love deep inside our being. Then we remember who we are and our desire to treat each other and ourselves with tenderness, care, and respect is revived.

Imagine how it might be if we choose to believe that everyone we meet along the path of life is our teacher of love and forgiveness. With this attitude, we could always find our way back to love and freedom. We would also find our way to all the noble virtues, such as peace, goodness, gentleness, and justice, for all virtues have their root and realization in love and forgiveness.

# 15

# Gratitude

It is a joy to be around people who sincerely bless and praise what is working in their life instead of lamenting over what isn't. No one exemplifies this more than the brilliant theoretical physicist Stephen Hawking. With his trademark wide grin, Hawking lives gratitude. Though he was permanently confined to a wheelchair by the time he was thirty-nine years old and barely able to communicate, he considered that fact not very important when measured against all his sources of joy and satisfaction.

Stricken with ALS (amyotrophic lateral sclerosis) in his early twenties, Hawking gradually lost control over his muscles until he could no longer walk, stand, or feed himself. Despite his severe disability, he has contributed more to scientific theory on the origin and evolution of the universe than any other person in the latter part of the twentieth century. Speaking once about his physical problems, Hawking said, "My advice to other disabled people is, concentrate on those things that you can do, and for which your disability is not a handicap. Above all, avoid making a profession of being disabled, with a permanent chip on your shoulder."

Stephen Hawking's advice could well apply to all of us, not just the disabled. Like Hawking, we need to look for all that is right with our life, to focus consciously with gratitude on those things that are working. We have the opportunity every day to choose what we focus on. We all know individuals who, no matter how fortunate, seem to focus on the negative. And we know individuals who, no matter how seemingly unfortunate, focus on the positive. The basic orientation to life of those individuals seems to be one of gratitude.

When we look for the good and praise it, and when we count our blessings, our focus is on what is right in life. Therefore, we feel more confident and optimistic, and our attention on negative situations and negative emotions is diminished. Our ability to enjoy life is greatly enhanced as we practice our ability to choose to focus on those things that evoke our sense of gratitude.

Sarah Ban Breathnach, author of *Simple Abundance,* has done much to promote the virtue of gratitude. Several years ago Breathnach appeared as a regular guest on the *Oprah Winfrey Show,* with Winfrey enthusiastically describing Breathnach's book as "life changing." Breathnach's suggestion to keep a gratitude journal and practice writing five things we are grateful for each day became a widely popular thing to do. Breathnach wrote, "You simply will not be the same person two months from now after consciously giving thanks each day for the abundance that exists in your life. And you will have set in motion an ancient spiritual law: the more you have and are grateful for, the more will be given to you."

When we infuse even the smallest amount of good in our life with our gratitude and attention, it will grow. Dwelling on the good in our life magnifies that good and serves as a magnet to attract even greater abundance. Not only does gratitude serve as a magnet to attract greater good, but it is also an important psychological strategy in everyday life, for gratitude helps us to be happier and healthier. Two psychologists, Michael E. McCullough and Robert A. Emmons, indicated the fact that gratitude promotes our happiness and well-being in a study. These two men conducted the Research Project on Gratitude and Thanksgiving.

The study required several hundred people in three different groups to keep daily dairies. The first group kept a diary of the events that occurred during the day, while the second group recorded their unpleasant experiences. The last group made a daily list of things for which they were grateful. The results of the study indicated that daily gratitude exercises resulted in higher reported levels of alertness, enthusiasm, determination, optimism, and energy. Additionally, the gratitude groups experienced less depression and stress, were more likely to help others, exercised more regularly, and made more progress toward personal goals. They were also more likely to feel loved. McCullough and Emmons also noted that gratitude encouraged a positive cycle of reciprocal kindness among people since one act of gratitude encourages another.

Perhaps making a daily list of things for which they were grateful promoted the participants' ability to be absorbed in life's daily activities with an increased awareness. Living in gratitude has much to do with living in a heightened state of awareness, taking the time to be aware of all the gifts that are ours to enjoy. Often we go through our busy and stressful days all but blind to the extraordinary beauty and abundance that surrounds us. How refreshing it is to slow down and wake up to the moment and to feel a sense of awe about life and its many blessings. Small, seemingly ordinary events can produce profound feelings of gratitude when we remain awake to the constant flow of good in our lives. Gratitude enables us to see the commonplace with new perceptions.

We can make it a practice every day to appreciate the commonplace. We can look for the magic and mystery in every moment. Life is full of children laughing, people helping, lovers smiling, animals playing, friends caring, and a world of other uplifting moments. Albert Einstein was a man who paid careful attention to his world, and he once said, "There are only two ways to live your life. One is as though nothing is a miracle; the other is as though everything is a miracle."

Just imagine how transforming it would be to live our

life as though everything were a miracle! Imagine taking the most ordinary moments and seeing them as something special. Most of us have certainly had these cherished moments, and in them, we discovered a sense of joy and wonder in just the simplest pleasures of everyday life. We may have been snuggled in our favorite spot on a brisk fall morning, sipping our first cup of coffee, or luxuriating in a majestic view of autumn leaves. Or we may have been looking into the eyes of a precious child and feeling overwhelmed with love and pride. On these, or other rich moments, our sense of being alive was renewed, and we were less likely to take things for granted.

In *Creation Spirituality,* Matthew Fox writes about how his experience with polio taught him the importance of not taking things for granted and instilled within him a deep sense of gratitude. Fox writes,

> When I was twelve years old, I had polio and could not walk for six months. The doctors could not reassure me that I would ever walk again. As it turned out, I did get my legs back. But I learned a lesson in the process that I have never forgotten: don't take anything for granted. I had taken my legs for granted, legs that work, legs that run and play ball, legs that take me exactly where I want to go. When my legs returned to me I was filled with gratitude— not gratitude for the "miracle" of my legs being healed, but rather gratitude for having legs at all, legs that work. I was filled with energy and promised myself that I would not waste my legs for as long as I lived.

Like Matthew Fox, we've all had experiences of losing something and then finding ourselves filled with a profound sense of gratitude upon its return. But we don't have to experience a great loss in order to become *consciously* grateful for the good in our life. We can choose to take the time to notice our blessings and to make it a habit to enjoy more fully what we already have. As we stop taking things for granted, we see what a miraculous gift life truly is, and we experience a completely new dimension of happiness.

However, sometimes we do get a wake-up call and realize how much we have taken for granted. Suddenly we have a sense of appreciation for everything that we have and for everything that we are, and our hearts are filled with thanksgiving for all those things great and small whose beauty and energy have enriched our life. We see the privileges of our life as gifts, not entitlements.

Sadly, there are people who possess little humility for the blessings in their lives—only a sense of entitlement. They have the mentality that life or someone owes them something regardless of what they may or may not have done to deserve it. An attitude of entitlement is devoid of any sense of gratitude, and it is an attitude that is repelling, for few traits are as distasteful to us as ingratitude. We have all felt the annoyance when people fail to verbalize gratitude for something significant that has been done for them. We find this sense of entitlement and "me-centered" approach to life unappealing and unacceptable. Typically accompanying this sense of entitlement and "me-centered" approach is the attitude that what they have is never enough or good enough. Poet Bertolt Brecht touched on this type of ingratitude when he wrote, "What a miserable thing life is: you're living in clover, only the clover isn't good enough."

When we look out and see only the negatives in our life and focus on what we think is missing, overlooking all the wonderful blessings we have, we risk being miserable, bitter people. We risk constantly comparing ourselves to others who have more, therefore, causing us to see our life and ourselves as lacking. I think perhaps it would serve us well to embrace the view of life that if we must compare, let us compare ourselves to those less fortunate.

Some years ago while vacationing in Hawaii, I found myself suddenly comparing myself to those who appeared less fortunate than me. I was touring the beautiful island of Oahu in a state of bliss to be enjoying such a paradise. We were passing miles and miles of pineapple fields en route to North Beach when suddenly I saw Filipino workers bent over in the hot sun planting. Our tour guide, Ralph, said they do that for almost twelve hours a day for very low wages. Then, as immigrant workers, they take their meager earnings and send it to their families back home. A heavy sadness hit my heart. It seemed unfair, a life of such backbreaking work and poverty in the midst of this paradise and affluence. The realization of the blessings in my own life struck me so profoundly. Tears streamed down my face as I felt such sorrow for the hard life of the workers coupled with the intense awareness of my own blessings. I didn't want someone else's suffering to be the wake-up call to my good fortune, but indeed it was.

I try to be wary of being so accustomed to having so much that the luxuries in my life feel like necessities and my privileges are seen as entitlements. The experience in Hawaii made me more aware that by the standards of many other countries in the world, most of us are unimaginably rich. Our very prosperity, however, threatens not only our capacity to give genuine thanks for our bounty, but unless we stay mindful, it has the potential to jeopardize our ability to be aware of our abundance.

Gregg Easterbrook has recently studied this particular problem associated with prosperity. His book *The Progress Paradox* focuses on statistical data indicating that Americans are better off than they were generations ago in terms of material goods and amount of free time available. However, surveys show the percentage of Americans who describe themselves as happy has not budged since the 1950s. Easterbrook argues that this has occurred due to abundance denial (meaning we just don't know how good we've got it) and choice anxiety (the stress created by having so many options). He notes that no matter how much we have, we never consider ourselves to be prosperous. He cites the fact that the majority of Americans envision only the rich as "well off" even though most Americans live relatively better than more than 99 percent of humans who ever lived. Easterbrook suggests that we need a "rebirth of thankfulness."

Easterbrook's findings point out that we often get so busy complaining, grumbling, and worrying that we forget all about the things for which we have to be grateful. Our well-worn patterns of fretting rob us of the moment's blessings and enjoyment of life. When we are worrying, it is difficult to see the positive side of things or the possibilities, but that is the very time to do so.

Millard Fuller, who founded Habitat for Humanity International, has been quoted as saying, "You can focus on the tremendous need and get discouraged or you can focus on what is going right, like building a house every fifty minutes." Such a perspective helps us keep our focus on the possibilities and opportunities in life even in the midst of great need.

Developing the habit to see the positive and possibility of things greatly contributes to our sense of well-being and freedom, as well as developing the habit of positive expectancy. We can begin each morning with an expectant mind, a mind that expects to see and experience all the good around us. We can be grateful for each new day and the unique potential that day holds. We can take the time to feel the magic and miracle of life that is there for us every second of every minute of every day.

Life is such a smorgasbord laden with more delicacies than we can possibly sample. Just acknowledging the wealth of opportunities before us can quickly put things in perspective. The poet Rumi wrote, "Every object, every being, is a jar full of delight. Be a connoisseur." Whether we are walking through the grocery store, completing a project at work, or reading a book, we can practice "being a connoisseur."

Practicing being a connoisseur was a lesson Dan Millman's mentor, nicknamed Socrates, wanted him to experience. Millman, author of *Way of the Peaceful Warrior,* described a time when Socrates challenged him to sit out on a large, flat stone until he had "something of value" to share. Dan sat out on the rock for hours and hours. On more than one occasion, believing he had come up with something, he went to tell Socrates. Each of these times, Socrates decided the statement was not good enough and sent Dan back to the rock for more hours of pondering. Finally, Dan had an insight that he knew was something of value. When he shared this insight, Socrates looked up, smiled, and welcomed Dan back inside. The "something of value" that Dan had realized was this: "There are no ordinary moments." This is the essence of gratitude. No moment, nothing in life, should be taken for granted. As we develop gratitude for every moment, even in times of challenge, we come to truly enjoy and appreciate life.

We can develop gratitude for even the difficult moments when we stay in touch with the idea that there is always more good going on in any situation than we are aware—that we can't yet know the greater good to which difficult circumstances might be leading. Paul the Apostle appeared to have this awareness when he wrote these lines while in a dark prison: "I have learned this one thing, that in whatever circumstances I am in, therein to be grateful."

I have a little book by Wallace D. Wattles that first introduced to me this idea of being grateful for all things. The pages are tattered and loose from all the readings through the years. The book actually contains two inspirational classics, *The Science of Getting Rich* and *The Science of Being Great.* My favorite chapter is the one on gratitude. Years ago, I wrote a quote from this chapter on an index card: "It is necessary, then, to cultivate the habit of being grateful for every good thing that comes to you, and to give thanks continuously. *And because all things have contributed to your advancement, you should include all things in your gratitude.*" To this day, I frequently read this quote and find that it immediately lifts my spirits and puts the events in my life in perspective.

This viewpoint was again reinforced to me some years ago when I attended a life, death, and transition workshop developed by Dr. Elisabeth Kübler-Ross. The workshop was an intensive weeklong experience that changed my life in many ways. One of the highlights of the week occurred when Dr. Kübler-Ross talked to us about being grateful for the challenges that have shaped our lives. "Should you shield the canyons from the windstorms," she reminded us, "you would never see the beauty of their carvings." Acknowledging the lessons our suffering has brought—the beauty of their carvings—is an important part of our healing journey. Doing so allows us to feel gratitude over what we have gained, instead of bitterness over what we've lost. As our recognition of our gains and gifts increases, old hurts of yesterday are healed and released.

As I look back upon my journey in life, I have come to appreciate all of my life's adventures, for the pain and struggles have brought with them the gifts of knowledge, wisdom, and compassion. My negative experiences allowed me to see and appreciate the gifts of life and to learn from them some of my greatest teachings. I feel like Winston Churchill must have felt when he said that he had a great appreciation of life because he had known "the deprivation of the trenches."

Now we don't have to live in the trenches to develop an appreciation for our blessings. We can just start by choosing to be grateful, and the more grateful we are for everything, the more reasons we find to be grateful. As we become increasingly grateful, we will notice that we become increasingly humble, as we realize that we cannot take full credit for our accomplishments and good fortune.

The more humble we become, the more we notice that we want to "give back" to the world. The gratitude and humility in our heart increases our desire to give to others and to help others fulfill their dreams and goals. We find that we want to reach out and help others who might be feeling down and unmotivated because we, too, have had those times. We know that to have someone show genuine interest, affirm our worth, and believe in us reignites our belief in ourselves and our enthusiasm for life.

Theologian Albert Schweitzer wrote, "At times our own light goes out and is rekindled by a spark from another person. Each of us has cause to think with deep gratitude of those who have lighted the flame within us." To have someone light the flame within us is a gift beyond measure. This flame allows us to view our potential.

Do you regularly acknowledge the people who have contributed to your success? Who lit the flame within you? Everyone likes to be acknowledged and appreciated. Tell others the reasons you appreciate them. Grace them with a sincere thank-you and watch their eyes dance with delight. We wouldn't be here without other people laboring to serve us. Can you think of one thing you did without the help of others?

Gratitude connects us to life and to the people who have been the vehicles for the good that has come to us. We exist in an interdependent world where everything and everyone is connected. There is no one, therefore, who does not owe a debt of gratitude to others. It is a wise person who is aware of their interdependence with others and who practices expressing their appreciation. Expressing our appreciation will bring the people in our life closer to us and contributes to the happiness of everyone.

Practice saying "thank you" more often, and the next time

you say "thank you" take the opportunity to transform something that can be mechanical into something real. Look the person in the eye and take a moment to be real and to make them real. Avoid making a trivial acknowledgment of something that lacks any real connection to feelings of gratitude. Also, take the time to appreciate other people's appreciation of you. Through the years, I've often received notes and calls from people who have attended my seminars or presentations expressing their gratitude. I try to just sit with these kind words and take them in with sincere appreciation.

Moreover, do not overlook taking the time to appreciate yourself and your own life's journey. Appreciate how far you've come and how much you've grown. There is great merit in appreciating and rejoicing in who you already are and what you already have and in taking the time to enjoy each success before immediately moving on to the next. Unfortunately, we often don't enjoy what we have because we are attached to an ideal of how it should be improved. We can pursue our goals while at the same time enjoying and appreciating what we already have.

Enjoying and appreciating what we have is living with an attitude of gratitude that is true wealth. Without a sense of gratitude, we are poor no matter what our net worth may be. Susan Jeffers writes in her book *End the Struggle and Dance with Life,* "No matter how many goodies are lavished upon us in life, unless we are grateful for them, we are still beggars at heart."

We can have the entire material good life can possibly offer, but if we are lacking in gratitude, we will not be happy. We will still be focused on what is missing. Our lack of gratitude will keep us in a state of misery and poverty and prevent us from being aware of the abundance of each moment. A great lifetime is nothing more than a series of great moments. A spirit of gratitude creates great moments. Through gratitude, we can develop an experience of true prosperity no matter what our level of income. We can choose to live each day with the most intense gratitude for even the smallest things.

As most of us have experienced, typically the smallest, most unexpected things bring us the greatest joy. We've all had those moments in which spontaneous waves of gratitude swept over us, and we are suddenly and magically shifted to a state of incredible love. Instantly our anxieties fade, and our frustrations are replaced with peace and contentment. I recall having such a moment when my son was a little boy, and we were having breakfast at a Cracker Barrel Old Country Store restaurant. Having finished his meal fairly quickly and with a little money in his pocket, he was eager to explore the gift area. Since I was positioned where I could keep an eye on him, I agreed to let him do so. A short time later, he came rushing back to the table with a big grin on his face. "Look what I got for you, Mama," he said while flashing a book in my face. Taking the book from his little hands, I read the title, *Mother, Thank You for All Your Love*. My son had spent almost every penny in his pocket on a sweet gift that expressed his love for me. To this day, my heart swells with unsurpassed gratitude. He is now twenty-nine years old, and I still keep this little treasure on my desk.

Other times I am flooded with sudden intense feelings of gratitude when I commune with nature. Nature has a joyous way of summoning my gratitude—a gentle breeze on a fall day, the rustling sound of a winding stream, a cricket's lullaby on a summer night, the sight of mountain peaks majestically rising, the crashing of waves on a quiet beach—how profoundly these speak to my heart. They seem to produce within me an overwhelming appreciation for the mysteries of life. The sights and sounds of nature make me feel like a happy child rejoicing in the magical world in which we live.

I remember rejoicing like a child the first time I saw Zion

National Park in Utah. As I gazed upon those mammoth vistas, my heart felt as though it was going to explode with gratitude. The spectacular landscape of massive sandstone cliffs, protruding rock formations, lush valleys enlivened by waterfalls and rivers—what stunning sculpture! I stood in awe and wonder, and that moment continues to be a peak experience I will never forget.

Whether it is in nature, or in our cozy bed, or sitting behind our computer, or wherever we are, we can cultivate the ability to feel profoundly grateful. Truly grateful people are grateful in all circumstances, and it does not seem to matter whether they are anywhere "special" or that anything "special" happens to them on any given day or not. Their gratitude seems to be rooted in remembrance, remembrance of all those who have loved them, of all the good they have, of all the gifts life offers. Gratitude is such a defining aspect of one's personality. A person's character can almost be identified by their attitude toward gratitude as well as their level of happiness. Think of people you regard as ungrateful, and you will quickly realize that not one of them is a happy person. Then, think of those people you know who express gratitude for even the smallest things. Chances are they are the people who come to mind as the happiest people you know.

Gratitude brings happiness and peace and wakes us up to a world of wonder and mystery. No wonder Saint Paul, in his first letter to the Thessalonians, urged us to "rejoice always" and "give thanks in all circumstances."

# 16

# Wealth and Money

Wealth is the ability to live well and freely. It is about abundant living in the fullest sense, flourishing, thriving, and growing in all areas of our life. There are many people with enormous amounts of money who live poorly and with very little freedom. Conversely, there are many people without great amounts of money living in modest yet comfortable circumstances who live well and feel free.

The ability to live well has much to do with our way of thinking, attitude, and focus. Our feelings of wealth often depend more on the extent of our focus than on our financial situation. When we focus on the positives in our life and all that we have, we feel wealthy. When we focus on what is missing, we feel deprived. In fact, we may be well-to-do in the external world, but if we are consistently focusing on what is missing, we are afflicted with poverty in our inner world. This feeling of deprivation may keep us on the treadmill of seeking things we believe will bring us the fulfillment we desire: a bigger house, a bigger car, a bigger wardrobe, a bigger income, and on and on.

The tendency to focus on what is missing typically comes from a feeling of emptiness, so we find ourselves spending money to fill up this sense of emptiness. We soon learn, however, that doing so only leaves us feeling emptier. The antidote for this consumerism is to explore our feelings and come to terms with what this emptiness is all about. Perhaps we feel a lack of purpose or that we are not "good enough." Feelings of not being "good enough" tend to compel us to compensate by accumulating things.

Whatever the feelings may be, using money as a quick fix is just that, a temporary solution.

Making the distinction between what external things can give us and what they can't is important, as well as understanding that our desire for "things" is actually the desire for the attribute of life those things represent to us. We may be seeking approval, admiration, power, recognition, or some other deeper need. Often we can obtain that sense of fulfillment by looking within ourselves without actually having to possess the "thing out there." Perhaps we don't have to own the biggest house in order to be admired, or the designer dress to get recognition, or be a member of a prestigious organization to feel important. Maybe we can give ourselves those feelings.

For many years, I've had the privilege of teaching self-development programs in the corporate world, and on a number of occasions, I have facilitated study groups on prosperity. More than once, I have seen participants shift from the belief that they needed more "money" to the realization that they needed to feel a greater sense of freedom and/or meaning in their life. I have seen people come to terms with the fact that money doesn't always represent wealth. They may possess an abundance of money yet are emotionally or spiritually poor or imprisoned by the demands their money requires. Some realize that chasing the dollar has robbed them of their joy, time, and energy, and they realize the price they have paid for their money in terms of their freedom or health.

As they began to see how it is possible to have money and not be truly wealthy, their desire for true wealth grew. They became less inclined to glamorize and seek their deepest gratification in the sheer making of money. Even though they continued to value money, they became less inclined to make the acquisition of money and power their total measure of success and more inclined to balance their lives with wealth in other areas. For some, there was the discovery that their inordinate emphasis on money had to do with their own issues of self-worth.

Glamorizing and seeking things in the external world is sometimes a sign of low self-worth. When we feel "less than," we often spend more than we have in order to feel like more, allowing consumerism and materialism to run our lives. On the other hand, low self-worth can also prevent us from allowing abundance into our life because we don't feel deserving. When we don't feel deserving, we can unconsciously block things and opportunities that come our way, or we can feel incapable of going after even the small things that we want.

Since true prosperity happens in our consciousness, a high sense of self-worth is essential in creating wealth. We have to find the gold in ourselves before we can truly strike it rich; our good doesn't come from the world around us, but from the world within us. True wealth comes from valuing and empowering our unique self and knowing that we are worthy and deserving. As our sense of value and self-worth rises, our expectations also percolate upward, and we begin to attract abundance in all areas of our life.

There is an old poem containing the lines "I bargained with life for a penny, and life would pay no more." As we grow in self-worth, we will find ourselves less willing to bargain with life for a penny, and we will discover that loving ourselves pays enormous dividends.

In my own life, things began to change significantly, as I gradually realized my problems with money had their roots in self-worth issues and in my early childhood experiences with money. My father was often unemployed due to chronic heart problems and money was scarce. He also drank, raged, and gambled excessively. My mother worked as a bookkeeper for modest wages and was the primary breadwinner of the family at a time when that wasn't a fashionable thing to do.

With my parents' constant struggle over the lack of

money, we endured crisis after crisis. The lack of money seemed to be a major contributor to the chaos in my home. As an adult, I found myself re-creating the crisis atmosphere around money that I had experienced as a child. Repeatedly I found myself struggling to pay my bills and to survive financially. So for most of my life, when it came to money, I was like an eternal adolescent hoping someone would rescue and take care of me because I truly didn't feel capable of taking care of myself. Of course, the tactic of being rescued only produced temporary results and always seemed to bring more pain into my life.

The suffering and humiliation around money issues was devastating. Struggling with poverty was like living with my spirit in bondage. Finally, I realized that I was poor on the outside primarily because I was poor on the inside. I felt unworthy of good things. In order to pull myself out of poverty, I had to empower myself with a sense of worth. The good news is that as I learned to love and value myself, my ability to create prosperity grew. The more I chose to think of myself, my ideas, and my service as valuable, the more others responded to that and willingly paid me well. Behind my financial issues were self-esteem and spiritual lessons to be learned.

Needless to say, limitation has been a powerful teacher for me. At the same time, to be on the receiving end of abundance and generosity has also been a powerful teacher. The life of a man I never knew was instrumental in further eradicating from my consciousness the negative associations I had with money. His name was W. K. Kellogg. Thanks to Kellogg's success in building a worldwide cereal industry, and then investing his fortune in a philanthropic foundation, I received a grant for $5,000 to further my education. This great gift came to me at a time when I was struggling as a single mother to break free of my own poverty consciousness and negative tapes about deserving or desiring wealth. Suddenly, I had a deep appreciation for how the success of one person could impact so profoundly the lives of millions. Kellogg wanted to use his wealth to bring "the greatest good to the greatest number," and he did just that. His dream continues to live through the lives of the countless people he has helped through his foundation.

To those whose beliefs about money have always been favorable and positive, it may seem strange that anyone could have negative associations toward this powerful resource. But indeed many people do. Not everyone sees money as a positive and powerful tool. Not everyone is comfortable with the thought of being wealthy. Some people believe that desiring a great deal of money makes them greedy or mercenary, or they have an underlying fear that financial success will cause them to compromise their values. Some people believe they will have to give up too much to have money; they associate money with a loss of freedom. They may believe that making more money means working around the clock or being tied to a job they don't like.

Some people believe it is unfair if they have abundance and others don't. This was certainly true for me. As my prosperity increased, however modest, a sense of guilt plagued me when I was around those less fortunate. Then one day I read a quote by the minister Eric Butterworth that shifted my thinking. Butterworth wrote, "When you breathe all the air you need, you can never deprive anyone else of all the air they are able to breathe." Abundance, like air, is unlimited.

Reflecting upon Butterworth's words helped me to realize that my abundance doesn't cut into anyone's supply. I began to comprehend that my being poor did not help one person to have more. The truth is there is an unlimited supply of success, and we can have all the success and abundance we want. Others cannot take away our success, and we cannot take away from others. There is enough for everyone.

However, if we are stuck in a scarcity consciousness, other people's successes can feel like a loss to us, and we develop an underlying resentment at the good fortune of others. This may even show up as sort of a reverse snobbery—obtaining a sense of virtue from having no money. Of course, some people were raised to believe that it is more holy to be poor.

Whatever the reasons, money tends to be an emotionally charged issue for most of us. For some, matters of money are matters of shame or guilt. It may be the shame of growing up poor, or the shame of not making as much money as we think we should be making, or the guilt of mishandling our finances, or the guilt that if we earn more someone else will miss out. The fact is that it will be very difficult to create more money in our life if the idea produces some sort of shame. A positive and creative attitude toward money is a must if we desire prosperity; to master financial success, we must have positive associations with money. One way to move toward associations that are more positive is to think of money as a means of acquiring good for yourself and others, as did W. K. Kellogg.

Though money doesn't necessarily bring happiness, the truth is that money is a powerful resource. It is a tool that not only helps us to live better, but one with which we can also help others live better. It is a tool that gives us the ability to positively impact the world by allowing us to perform wonderful philanthropic and generous acts that enrich lives.

John Paul DeJoria is a man who seems to understand that wealth is a source of happiness when used to enrich our own lives as well as the lives of others. DeJoria, the cofounder and CEO of John Paul Mitchell Systems, is a caring humanitarian whose rags-to-riches story is truly inspiring. The son of immigrant parents, DeJoria was at one time a member of a Los Angeles street gang who found himself homeless on more than one occasion. After his remarkable turnaround and rise to fortune, he has contributed millions of dollars to charitable causes. One of his many charitable endeavors has been helping to save a tribe of more than two thousand Native Americans living in the mountains near the Mexican border from near extinction by providing food, blankets, plows, and seeds. John Paul DeJoria truly lives his philosophy: "Success unshared is failure." This sharing of success is the ideal goal of an abundance of money—to increase the quality of life for everyone, to make our dreams and the dreams of others come true.

There are few of us who can make our dreams come true and develop our highest potential while carrying the weight of poverty. Most of our goals in life require money, and, in fact, there is very little in our culture that isn't impacted by the energy of money. So while we know that money is not the game of life, we know it is definitely a very important aspect. One of the primary urges of life is to be affluent—to be in the flow of abundance, which allows us the personal freedom to function easily, accomplish worthwhile purposes, and grow.

The word "affluence" means literally to "free flow." One of the most powerful ways to create the "flow" is by giving. In life, we need to give whatever need we want to receive. Whether it is more money that we need, or love, or help, or companionship, we need to give it. And we need to give in the spirit of truly wanting to help, of truly wanting to be of service. If we give only to be rewarded, our motive is not a healthy one. Giving with the expectation of receiving is like a manipulation. It simply doesn't work when we give with one hand and wait to receive with the other.

A beautiful example of a person truly wanting to help is Oseola McCarty, the washerwoman who in 1995 donated $150,000 of her life savings to finance scholarships for African American students at the University of Southern Mississippi. McCarty, who had to quit school after the sixth grade, always believed in the importance of education and deeply wanted to provide others with the opportunity she missed. "You give it because you want to give it," she said, "I wanted to share it with somebody." Her generosity inspired others to match her donation, and the scholarship fund has tripled and is still growing, forever changing the lives of its recipients. Her book *Oseola McCarty's Simple Wisdom for Rich Living* has inspired thousands of people. She is indeed a remarkable example of a person living to give instead of living to get.

Like Oseola McCarty, by involving ourselves in acts of goodwill that contribute to the well-being of others, we can all be philanthropists. We can all give our time, talents, and some portion of whatever money we have. But not only do we need to give, we also need to receive with gratitude and grace, for receiving is part of the circulation—a part of keeping the flow going. Moreover, if we receive with a sincere feeling of gratitude and joy, things will continue to come our way.

I remember once when I found myself on the receiving end of a very loving act. My son was about ten years old when we experienced yet another evening when I was low on cash. We were riding along in the car pooling our resources so we could stop at the grocery store and buy "something" for his breakfast. With amusement, I counted out $0.38; he had $1.78. I said, "Justin, we are just out of everything but waffles for your breakfast. Why don't you get a small bottle of syrup for your waffles?" He quickly asked, "Well, what about your coffee; you don't have any coffee." I said, "That's okay, I'll get some coffee at work. We need to get something for you." "Okay," he replied, "I'll get a small bottle of syrup."

Well, I waited and waited. Finally, I saw him at the checkout with a small package in his hand. Then he came running to the car, hopped in, flashed his hand open, and proudly presented me with a small bag of gourmet coffee.

"Sorry I took so long Mommy, but I was trying to find this coffee for you." Tears flooded my eyes. "But what about your syrup," I asked. "Oh, I'll just find something to eat; I wanted you to have your coffee."

It is difficult to imagine that at that moment my son felt any greater joy than I did; yet, I know the gifts and benefits we receive from giving far exceed anything we get in return. I know his little heart was filled with the same happiness he brought me, for what we give, we simultaneously receive.

Of course, the more we have, the more we can give. So how do we bring more money into our lives? How do we prevent ourselves from having to decide between a small bag of coffee and a bottle of syrup? As I mentioned earlier, the starting point of all riches is the development of a high sense of self-worth and value. This leads to a prosperity consciousness—a consciousness that sees life's resources and possibilities as unlimited and available for all—including us.

Cultivating a prosperous consciousness means embracing the awareness that the universe is fundamentally abundant and understanding that it is not the world that restricts what we can have; it is our belief about what we can have that restricts our abundance. Cultivating a prosperous consciousness means uncovering a new image, a new belief system about who we are and what we can have and do. It means clearing out poverty-oriented thinking patterns and releasing self-limiting ideas.

We must clear out poverty-oriented thinking, because to become rich, we have to think rich. We have to develop the habit of thinking abundantly and consistently hold the idea of wealth and success in our mind. We have to think about and visualize our goals as realities until we impress upon our mind an unshakable belief that we can and will achieve them—realizing that we can only receive what we see ourselves receiving.

We must shift our attention to focusing with a grateful heart on what we have and what we desire rather than on what we perceive we're missing. Focusing on the absence of a thing in our life will not let more of that thing in. It may not be easy to get beyond focusing on limitations while we are still experiencing scarcity, but it must be done. We naturally attract the material conditions that correspond to our thoughts and emotions. What we think about comes about; whatever we focus our thoughts on expands. If we persistently talk about not having enough, not having enough is what we will experience.

The abundance in our life is simply the outer manifestation of our inner state of consciousness. Our lives mirror our consciousness, and the abundance in our life is but another mirror to reveal what is going on within our own mind. We have to uncover the correlation between what we are thinking and speaking and what we are getting to begin talking and thinking about only what we desire. Discrimination in selecting our words must be employed, and we must refuse to speak words that have in them the idea of poverty.

Perhaps it is becoming clear that the most difficult obstacles to overcome in having what we want are the internal ones. Unfortunately, many people believe they do not have the money they desire because they are unlucky. That is like shutting ourselves in a closet and vowing there is no sunshine. The problem is our belief system. When we believe something, we subconsciously begin collecting evidence to support our belief, and sooner or later, whatever we intensely believe becomes our reality. To become prosperous, we must develop a belief system that knows it is possible. One of the ways we can develop an empowering belief system around money is to intensify our desire to generate a greater income.

Desire—not just wishing, but a keen pulsating desire— is the mind's mechanism for starting action. A clear picture of what a greater monetary income would mean to you generates this desire. The clearer your connection between the money you desire and the fulfillment of your deepest dreams, the more desire will be generated. A powerful way to make this connection is to write down all the things money will do for you and then generate the feeling state of having more money and the fulfillment it will bring. Desire motivates us to plan definite ways to increase our financial prosperity, but desire alone will not change our financial condition. We must establish the intention to change it. Intention is a commitment to bring into existence a particular result. Our intention creates a conduit of energy that has organizing power and establishes a direction. When we have a clear intention, we generate energy that is focused like a laser beam to manifest what we want. Our intention informs the energy that flows through us; it sets the energy into motion.

Since we are in charge of our intentions and they originate within us, intention involves the use of our will. We must choose our intentions according to the outcomes we desire to produce, for intentions produce specific effects. Ambivalence and resistance disturb intention. The less ambivalence and resistance there is, the less delay between the establishing of the intent and the receiving of it. Establish the intention to manifest what you desire and get in the total feeling state of having what you want. Once you've launched your intention, you have to match your feeling state to it; you have to set your receiver to that channel. You must be in the mode to receive what you are asking. In addition, you must use your imagination to visualize having what you deeply desire. As you do so, you begin to harmonize with it, thus, bringing the feeling of having it into your present reality. This feeling begins to draw it to you. The more you concentrate on your positive intentions, the quicker your old images of lack and limitation will fade, and they will hold less power over you.

After you have focused your attention on what you want, have generated a keen pulsating desire for that outcome, and established a clear intention, the next step is to take the intention and launch a goal from it. For example, if your intention were to generate a certain amount of income for a given year, what goal would satisfy that intention? Perhaps you would need to establish certain goals regarding the number of new clients you would need, or a new level of service you would provide, or new contacts you would need to make. Goals are about applying action to your intentions.

Progress depends on clear, specific, well-defined goals designed around your intentions. Each specific goal needs a systematic action plan. Next, you must be willing to do what it takes to make it happen, taking steps daily to materialize your goals. As you do, you will notice each success generates momentum for the next.

However, a phase may come when you do not have any outer evidence that your diligent inner work is paying off. Remember that it takes time for the new to come and realize that some of your earlier thoughts of lack and limitation may still be creating your reality. Don't give up! Gradually, you will experience the results of your new thinking. Keep in mind that prosperity is a process. With your shift of awareness, your desires will come true.

Of course, some very practical things must be handled to create the prosperity you desire. Consider the following questions: Are you intelligently using the money that is flowing through your life? Are you paying off your debts in a timely manner? Paying debts is one of the primary requisites of becoming prosperous. Is your money working for you (such as investments) or against you (such as credit card debt)? Are you saving? A commitment to save is an investment in self-worth. In addition, money saved gives you options. Are you having some fun with your money? Money is for fun as well as paying bills; otherwise, you lose your enthusiasm. However, this doesn't mean you blindly give in to all your desires. Balance is the key.

By changing your beliefs about money as well as taking positive steps, you will find a path to greater prosperity. The experience of learning to create abundance is a process of growth that involves an opportunity to change and expand not only your beliefs about money, but about life. It may lead you to understand how your consciousness is the creator of all of your experiences. It may also lead you to believe, as it has for me, that abundance is not something you acquire, but something you tune into. Everything you desire is there just waiting for you when you recognize that the world is abundant with ample resources.

Money is a tool that has the potential to set us free to live better and give more. By having a healthy attitude toward money and using our creative mind to produce valuable ideas and to be of service, we will thrive. As we grow, contribute, and find even more ways to be useful to the world, our wealth will increase. In the meantime, we need to live generously and joyfully with the money we have. Before we can expect more, we must give thanks for that which we already have. As we do, our abundance will increase, for blessing our supply increases its flow.

# 17

# Faith, Spiritual Growth, and Prayer

Every great success story is a story of faith. When great faith stirs within us, we find ourselves moving forward with confidence and conviction. We are full of positive expectancy and demonstrate great power. In fact, throughout the ages, faith has been recognized as a power. Saint Paul put it right up there as one of the three great words with power: *faith*, hope, and love.

The works of our faith can radically change our lives and the lives of others. Through his faith, Mahatma Gandhi was able to unite India and free his people from British rule. The faith of Mother Teresa enabled her to establish the Missionaries of Charity, now an order of more than four thousand nuns running orphanages, AIDS hospices, and other charity centers throughout the world. Rosa Parks's faith gave her the courage to refuse to give up her bus seat to a white man, which led to the Montgomery bus strike, the first large-scale, organized protest against segregation using nonviolent tactics.

With the power of their faith, Gandhi, Mother Teresa, and Rosa Parks took action and overcame tremendous odds. Each of these individuals believed they were connected to a power much greater than their own that could see them through, and this was the foundation of their faith. Their faith gave them a sense of hope, courage, and the positive expectancy that they could handle the outcomes their actions might generate.

As we can see from these great leaders, faith is not passive. Faith is not about just "hoping" things will work out and just waiting to see what happens. It is about taking, in faith, whatever step is possible today to move us toward our commitments. Then each day, we take another faithful step. As Dr. Martin Luther King Jr. said, "Take the first step in faith. You don't have to see the whole staircase, just take the first step." As we step forward, our faith in what is possible increases—our persistent action backed by our total commitment pumps up our faith.

As our faith is pumped up, so is our courage. We find our doubt and fear gradually dissolving, and we come to believe that good things will unfold for us regardless of appearances and obstacles. This powerful state of mind begins to transform our ideas and dreams into realities, for our believing opens the way for our receiving. We begin to attract into our lives that which we believe, and we discover for ourselves what the ancient teachings tell us: "It is done unto you as you believe," and "If you have faith as a grain of mustard seed, you will say to this mountain, 'Move from here to there,' and it will move; and nothing will be impossible to you."

Tyrone "Muggsy" Bogues chose to believe that nothing is impossible. Standing at only 5'3" tall, with the dream of playing basketball in the National Basketball Association, he was often discouraged by others who reminded him that the overwhelming majority of male players in the NBA were above 6'3". Yet, Bogues, with a trusting and believing attitude, refused to believe what others told him was "impossible." He became the shortest player ever to play in the NBA. That fact alone is an amazing accomplishment, but the sports arena hasn't been Bogues's only challenge. Growing up in a Baltimore ghetto where violence was common, he faced many challenges in his early years, including being accidentally shot in the arm at the age of five. Nevertheless, through his mother's unconditional love and encouragement, he rose above his surroundings and learned to believe in himself and to have faith.

Today, after fourteen years in the NBA, Bogues is one of the most admired and inspiring men in basketball, on and off the court. Through his Always Believe Foundation, which supports programs for disadvantaged populations, he is helping others to have a better life. Muggsy Bogues shows us how much can be achieved if we believe and possess a faith of positive expectancy despite all odds.

Not only must we believe and have faith that we will receive, but also we must ask for those things we deeply desire. So often, the things we want in our life elude us because we don't ask for them. The barriers to asking for what we want may be rooted in fear, limited thinking, not realizing what is available to us, or in simply not knowing what we want. There are many dynamics contributing to our failure to ask. However, to manifest our desires, we must ask—we must ask believing, accepting, and trusting that we will receive. If we are lacking in any one of these attitudes, which are the very foundation of faith—belief, acceptance, and trust—our faith is weakened.

For many of us our weak link is trusting; we want to control instead of trust. However, we discover that as we learn to live with a more trusting attitude, we feel stronger and more resourceful, and we have a sense of guidance. With a trusting attitude, we find ourselves struggling less with fear and anxiety; therefore, we are less inclined to obsess about everything in our life. We also discover that unimaginable doors open, enabling us to find our way through whatever challenge we are facing. These seemingly miraculous occurrences generate hope and expectancy and help us to appreciate the mysteries of life.

George Lucas is a man who appreciates and contemplates the mysteries of life. His science-fiction saga *Star Wars* spread the concept of "using the Force"—that vast reservoir of energy that is the ground of our being. In an interview with Bill Moyers, Lucas stated,

I put the Force into the movie in order to try to awaken a certain kind of spirituality in young people, more a belief in God than a belief in any particular religious system. I wanted to make it so that young people would begin to ask questions about the mystery. Not having enough interest in the mysteries of life to ask the question, 'Is there a God or is there not a God?'—that is for me the worst thing that can happen.

Asking questions about the mysteries of life, about the invisible realities, educates us and leads us to examine our beliefs about a "Higher Power." Many of us have struggled with understanding that which we cannot see, clearly define, or prove scientifically. We have struggled with relying upon a power we don't fully understand. Perhaps it might serve us to remember the advice of Thomas Edison when he was once asked to define electricity. Edison responded, "No one really knows what it is; only what it does. But it exists. Use it!" Edison succinctly pointed out that until we consciously use electricity, we will not experience its power or its ability to do anything useful for us. But when we do use it, we have absolutely no doubt about its existence.

Many of us have had the same experience in connecting to a Higher Power or God or whatever we might want to call that unnamable mystery. Until we consciously chose to connect with that power, we did not have the experience of knowing it. But once we did connect, we felt convicted that there is an intelligence at work that is far greater than anything we can comprehend. We then came to believe in the invisible as readily as we accept the physical, and as we did, we felt ourselves becoming more trusting and optimistic.

Optimism is a definite characteristic of a person with faith, for true optimism is a natural outcome of seeing ourselves as expressions of God, a God who wants only our good. Iyanla Vanzant, author of numerous bestsellers, including *Acts of Faith,* is a remarkable example of a woman whose life has been transformed by her faith in God. This faith created within her a spirit of optimism and a passion to develop her spiritual awareness. Born to an unwed mother, raised by abusive relatives and family friends, married to a man who beat her, and becoming a single mother who went on welfare to help support her three children, Vanzant relied on her faith to change her life. She worked her way through college and law school, and then wrote books. "Spiritual consciousness does not make your problems go away," she says. "It does, however, help you view them from a different vantage point."

We can discover, as Vanzant did, that developing a spiritual consciousness enables us to see our problems from a different perspective—the perspective that our problems are opportunities to look inward, to heal our insecurities and wounds, and to choose to move forward in faith. A spiritual consciousness, a consciousness that knows there is an extraordinary, unending spiritual force of love that continually sustains us, gives us strength to face our fears and discover that life is here to support us.

Sadly, many of us have accepted the prevailing notion that the world is a dangerous and unsafe place. Therefore, we allow ourselves to drift in a sea of pessimism and helplessness; thus, we are filled with fear. We approach life with a negative expectation when we are filled with fear, for fear is a product of negative expectation. Much of my life's journey has been transforming myself from a person who moved through life with an ever-present fear to a person who chooses to have faith. This has been an enormous challenge because, having covered my negative thinking with convincing platitudes, I had fooled even myself about the subtle pessimism that permeated my thinking. In hindsight, I can see that I was just denying my fear, which only caused it to go deeper underground.

For example, I was always denying my fear of lacking the financial ability to take care of myself in the world. To admit that I felt incompetent, insecure, and helpless in this area felt humiliating, so I would cover those feelings up with a false bravado.

Finally, I stopped rejecting my fear and chose to examine it compassionately. Examining my fear allowed me to establish a new belief system about myself and gave me the freedom to choose faith over fear. Before I developed the awareness that I had the power to choose faith, I would read stories of people with great faith and say, "Gosh, I wish I was like that." But the problem was I couldn't see myself truly being like that, because my whole being was filled with such anxiety. Not that I didn't try. I was often on my knees begging, or running around saying affirmations, or reading the Bible and other spiritual literature. I just couldn't seem to find the magic key that unlocked the door to a life filled with faith and peace.

Eventually, I stopped looking for a magic key. I just took on the task of breaking the negative, fearful habits of thinking that were deeply ingrained in my consciousness one step at a time. I began to accept that the creative power of the universe was within me. I began to affirm a favorable outcome for everything I planned or did. I began to cultivate my faith in a divine, infinite intelligence and allowed it to invigorate and strengthen my imagination. I found it opened my mind to more expanded ideas. I also found that faith is something I must choose every day, and as I do, I am filled with the expectation of a positive outcome. Choosing faith also fills me with enthusiasm, energy, and a vibrant feeling of optimism. On those days when the old fears pop up, I have a new awareness that I control how long I ruminate about those fears. I control whether to choose to expect good things or bad things. As I break free of my habit of negative expectation, much of my anxiety falls away.

In facing and learning to deal with my fears, I realized that some of my fears had to do with my misconceptions of the nature of God. When I was young, I heard more preaching about God's judgment than God's love. I do not recall being told that my goodness was just as intrinsic as my "sinner" self, or the worst aspects of my being. I believed in a God who offered or withheld blessings by virtue of my behavior. I grew up thinking of God as a person who loved me when I was good and who got angry with me when I was bad. These early experiences generated feelings of guilt, shame, judgment, and fear and certainly did not program me to think about my worth.

As I matured and searched for my own truth, I found an understanding of God that was meaningful to me and a God that supported my sense of worth. This God wasn't way up in the sky or separate from me, but a presence in the depths of my soul. Perhaps my experience is best described in the words of Ralph Waldo Emerson: "When we have broken with the God of tradition, and ceased from the God of the intellect, then God fires us with his presence."

Fired with the presence of God, I began to identify myself more with that presence and to see myself as an eternal soul with a body—a recognition that I am in material form, but I am a part of what is formless. I experienced a knowingness that my deeper self is a spiritual self that is connected to everything. I understood that we are one with each other, one with the absolute, and that our consciousness is contained in a sea of consciousness. I came to view God as the infinite intelligence that created and sustains everything in existence—the limitless source of all. I began to see each one of us as God's possibility for expressing God, with each of us having the opportunity to be the arms and legs of God.

On an episode of *The Oprah Winfrey Show*, I listened to the story of two people who I think embody the arms and legs of God, Trong and Rani Hong. Their story, as individuals and as a couple, is truly amazing. Only an unbending faith could have allowed them to survive and, now, to thrive in the most astounding way. As a young boy of nine, Trong lived in a cave for two years after his parents put him on a ship to save him from being a child soldier in Vietnam. After witnessing unspeakable brutality and enduring the most depraved conditions imaginable, Trong found himself shipwrecked on a small island. He found shelter in a cave and lived there with monkeys as his only companions until he was rescued two years later.

Rani came to this country form Southern India where she was a victim of the child-trafficking industry. She was so severely beaten and bruised by the traffickers that she appeared physically and mentally ill. At the age of eight, Rani was freed through an adoption, which brought her to the United States. Rani recalls her adoptive mother reading the Bible to her every day. This act taught her to believe. She was particularly fond of reading—"Ask and you shall receive." Rani grew up developing the faith her adoptive mother taught her.

Trong and Rani met on a blind date, married, and went on to create tremendous success in their life. One of their great successes is the founding of the Tronie Foundation, which is dedicated to ending human trafficking and building shelter projects in the United States and abroad. The faith of these remarkable people not only altered the course of their individual lives, but also allowed them to contribute to the world in a remarkable way.

Like Trong and Rani, we can also contribute to the world in a remarkable way. As we cultivate our faith and consciously pursue our spiritual growth, we will experience tremendous inner growth, and we will evolve. As a result of this inner growth, we will find ourselves reaching out to others more and more, becoming even greater instruments for the healing of this world.

So what would motivate us to pursue consciously our spiritual growth? Many of us reach a point on our journey for success when we realize we have attained the majority of our goals and have become a better person for all that we have been doing, but we are still not fulfilled. This insight that something is missing sets us on a new kind of search—a search for spiritual sustenance. This search often leads us to asking questions about God and fills us with a desire to know God. This quest is as old as recorded history and can be found in every civilization.

Asking questions about God can simply be an intellectual exercise that doesn't necessarily lead to knowing God. The only way to know God is to discover God within our own consciousness. The deep profound feeling of being one with God can't be communicated; it can only be experienced through communing with God. As we commune with God, we begin to bring the insightful knowledge and guidance from our soul into our human personality. As we do so, we will be led to the blossoming of our full potential in all areas of our life. We will discover that the greatest journey we can ever make is the journey of our soul back to its source.

When we journey back to our source and experience our oneness with God, we move through the world differently. We find ourselves more compassionate, giving, and caring, because we feel our oneness with everything. We feel who we are beyond name and form. Thus, we become less identified with the psychodynamics of our personality and less willing to create or become involved with superficial drama.

To develop our relationship with the divine presence within, we can use certain tools of spiritual practice like prayer and meditation. Both prayer and meditation are powerful methods of connecting with our source and our inner self and shifting our attention from the conditions around us to deeper levels of our being. They build a deep abiding faith in that which cannot be seen but which produces everything that is seen. They bring God alive in our own personal experience. We can think of prayer as an intimate, ongoing communication with God, a God-directed thought which spiritualizes our thoughts. Meditation is the experience of feeling our oneness with God and listening.

For a large part of my life, prayer was about asking a distant deity to do me a favor. Sometimes, it was about begging for help. Most of my prayers were uttered in fear, not in confidence. I've learned to pray differently. I have moved away from anxiously imploring or trying to influence or appease God. My prayers now are more about affirming my oneness with the divine presence and my desire to align myself with divine purpose, power, and wisdom. They are also about expressing gratitude and a reverence for all of creation.

Though there are times when I pray with a nagging fear, more often I pray with a sense of expectancy. Reflecting upon my life experiences, I repeatedly see how expectation and acceptance are synonymous. I see that what I accepted in consciousness, I received. So I now pray with an expectant frame of mind. When I hear people say that they have prayed over and over again, but their prayers have not been answered, I wonder about any beliefs, attitudes, and self-concepts that might be blocking their prayers. If we are serious about what we are praying for, we need to do everything possible to transform our consciousness to make it happen, to align ourselves with our greater good. Often this means developing an entirely new self-image.

Meditation supports us in developing a new self-image; it allows us to experience our oneness with God and to know who we truly are. As a result, a new way of seeing and knowing ourselves is aroused. We also begin to experience directly that we are not our thoughts, but that thoughts occur within us. So if we've had thoughts that support a negative self-image, we realize that we are free to change those thoughts. Meditation has the power to dissolve the mental images with which we have identified and to hear our own inner wisdom about who and what we are. It is an opportunity to turn off those fearful mind movies and that noisy internal dialogue and reach a state of letting go.

Meditation is a state of "being," not an act of "doing." Meditation is not about trying to get into God or to get God into us. It is to "be still, and know that I am God" (Psalms 46:10)—to experience our oneness with God. To meditate is like flowing beyond the boundaries of our ego and merging into an at-one-ment, awareness that there is no demarcation between God and us. It allows us moments of transcending any sense of separation.

Whether through prayer, meditation, or just simply having time for quiet, it is essential to take time each day to recharge our spiritual batteries. We are living in the most rapidly changing world in the history of humankind; we are on an accelerated path. Without quiet interludes, we can become overwhelmed and anxious and experience life more as an arduous adventure than the miraculous journey that it truly is. We can miss participating consciously in the unfolding of our own personal expression of divinity, which is the true meaning of success.

To unfold our own personal expression of divinity means acknowledging that we are spiritual beings evolving through an earthly experience and allowing spiritual growth to be the meaning and purpose of our life. With spiritual growth as the meaning and purpose of our life, we contribute to the peace of the world. Former secretary-general of the United Nations Dag Hammarskjöld is often quoted as having said, "We can only succeed in achieving world peace if there is a spiritual renaissance on this planet."

A spiritual renaissance on the planet will occur when

significant numbers of individuals commit to raising their own level of consciousness, for the collective consciousness of the world reflects the state of our individual levels of consciousness. To choose to live a life filled with faith certainly raises our individual consciousness and moves the world toward a spiritual quantum leap.